# AMERICAN LANGUAGE REPRINTS

VOL. 8

# A
# DICTIONARY
# OF
# POWHATAN

compiled by
William Strachey

With two word-lists of
Virginia Algonquian from other sources.

Evolution Publishing
Bristol, Pennsylvania.

Reprinted from:

William Strachey. 1849. *The Historie of Travaile into Virginia Britannia* (reprint of the 1624 edition). London:Hakluyt Society.

Anonymous [Gabriel Archer?]. 1860. "A relatyon of the Discovery of our River, from James Forte into the Maine" American Antiquarian Society, *Archaeologia Americana* IV.

Robert Beverley. 1705. *The History and Present State of Virginia.* London.

©1999 Evolution Publishing

First published 1999
Reprinted 2005

Printed in the
United States of America

*Dedicated to the memory of Frank T. Siebert, Jr.*

ISBN 1-889758-62-0

# CONTENTS

Preface by Frederic W. Gleach ........................................... 1

Excerpt from
the Historie of Travaile into Virginia Britannia ............... 9

Powhatan — English ...................................................... 15

English — Powhatan ...................................................... 61

Numerical Table .............................................................. 97

A Powhatan Word-list .................................................... 101

A Word-list of the Virginia Indians .............................. 105

Classification of the Eastern Algonquian Languages ... 107

# Preface to the 1999 Edition

The Powhatan tribes, a confederation of tribes led by the chief of the same name, were the original inhabitants of the area in which the Jamestown colony was settled in 1607, in the first permanent English colony in the New World. These tribes spoke several dialects (see Gerard 1904; Geary 1953; Siebert 1975:287-88, 195-96) of a language that became known to the Euroamericans as "Powhatan," now recognized as an Eastern Algonquian language (Goddard 1978) although previously classified with the Central Algonquian group (Michelson 1933, Bloomfield 1946). The Eastern Algonquian group also includes the languages of neighboring Algonquian groups, such as Nanticoke and the Unami and Munsee languages of the Delawares (or Lenni Lenape), and likely included the North Carolina Algonquian languages, although these are too poorly recorded to discuss with any certainty. The southern end of the distribution of Eastern Algonquian languages, below the Delawares, is generally poorly documented; this is due to a variety of factors including the interests and talents of the early writers in this area as well as the early dates of contact and policies of removal, isolation, and deculturation applied to these groups. While some of these languages from North Carolina, Virginia, Maryland, and Delaware were completely lost, or nearly so, Powhatan was at least partially recorded in the first decades of colonization, and a few brief word-lists were compiled at later dates. The best known of the early recordings of Powhatan, Captain John Smith's vocabulary, was published in 1997 as Volume 4 of this series, but the dictionary compiled by William Strachey, presented here, is considerably more extensive.

Producing a useful edition of early colonial attempts to record Native American languages always raises certain questions and problems pertaining to transcription, but Strachey's dictionary is a particularly difficult case. Three copies of his manuscript *The Historie of Travaile into Virginia Britannia* are known, but none are in his own hand: a copy presented to Sir Allen Apsley is now in the Bodleian Library at Oxford; one presented to Henry Percy, Ninth Earl of Northumberland, is now at Princeton; and one presented to Sir Francis Bacon is now in the British Library. The first two were probably produced around 1612, and the last around 1618 (Strachey 1953: xv-xvii, xxvi-xxvii, xxix). Only two of these, the Bodleian and the British Library copies, include the dictionary, but there are numerous small discrepancies between the two, and there are a number of entries in the Bodleian copy that are not in the British Library copy. Reconciling these to produce anything approaching an "authoritative" version is a Herculean task. This edition, which does not claim to be authoritative but is hoped to make the texts more readily available, is based on the British Library copy, with additions from the Bodleian manuscript where relevant. The British Library copy was published in 1849, and the Princeton copy was published in 1953; this latter edition included both versions of the dictionary in two-column parallel printing. A facsimile of the Bodleian copy of the dictionary has also been published, with transcription (Harrington 1955), making it easier to check the earlier versions—but also demonstrating the difficulty of that process. These manuscripts were produced by professional copyists, but even the finest hand from the early seventeenth century leaves many characters that cannot be transcribed with certainty—and this was true even for their contemporaries, as can be seen in the inconsistencies of different copies. The most common mistakes confuse -*m*-, -*w*-, -*in*-, and/or -*ni*-, and -*c*-, -*i*-, -*r*-, -*t*-, -*s*-, and -*x*-, but there are many others; when working with multiple copies of early seventeenth-century documents one quickly becomes used to these copyists' mistakes, and notices the spaces left and later filled in where the copyist had questions from the original.

The transcription from manuscript to print is, however, the second (and less problematic) transcription involved in the production of this document. Strachey, an Englishman who was not fluent in any Algonquian language, had to first record the Powhatan words themselves, transcribing the sounds using his English alphabet. When Strachey arrived at Jamestown in 1610—he had been aboard the *Sea Venture*, which went aground in the Bermudas and was delayed, the story of which provided the background for Shakespeare's *The Tempest*—he was probably better prepared for this task than was Captain John Smith; he had at least some education at Cambridge, and was probably personally acquainted with Thomas Hariot, who "spake the Indian language [North Carolina Algonquian]" (Strachey 1953: xxxi-xxxii, 21-22). As secretary of the colony Strachey might also be expected to have had more time to devote to the study of the Powhatan language than Smith did, although perhaps not as much direct interaction with the Powhatans. He used a variety of unusual vowel strings trying to capture the sounds; consonant doubling and *-hp-*, *-ht-*, and *-hk-* forms, perhaps to indicate a short preceding vowel (Geary 1953: 209); and whereas Smith made liberal use of terminal *-gh-* (to record a final sound that remains ambiguous), in Strachey's dictionary we see final *-wh* and *-h*. Clearly these English speakers had particular difficulty with Algonquian vowels and especially vowel finals; but, as with Smith, Strachey at least recognized not only these, but the often unstressed initial vowels in Algonquian languages, recording them variously as *U-*, *O-*, and *A-*. The spelling peculiarities and orthographic difficulties of Elizabethan English in general are thus compounded by efforts to record unfamiliar phonetic sequences. The Strachey dictionary cannot be used alone in trying to study the language, but used in conjunction with knowledge of other Eastern Algonquian languages and with the work on proto-Algonquian (e.g. Aubin 1975, Hewson 1993; see also regular contributions in the *Papers of the Algonquian Conference* series) some studies are possible, as Siebert (1975) demonstrated over 20 years ago. Recent research (eg., Feest 1990; Gleach 1997; Rountree 1989, 1990) has focused much more heavily on cultural and historical questions than on linguistic concerns, and it would be nice to see new students approach the language.

The remaining two pieces included in this volume offer only small glimpses of the language. The first is a list of Powhatan words included in a brief narrative of a 1607 exploring party up the James River, probably written by Gabriel Archer (Barbour 1969: 81, n.3), first examined by Mook (1943). The second is taken from the first relatively scholarly history of Virginia, by Robert Beverley (the accessible edition is Beverley 1947). This source is particularly important as it demonstrates the continued use of the language and of traditional practices at this time; Beverley also described a temple-house (*quioccasin*) he entered. It is now known that the language continued in some use well into the nineteenth century, and some traditional beliefs and practices even to the present, but this had to be established in the face of opinions such as Thomas Jefferson's that they had "lost their language" (Jefferson 1955:97) in the eighteenth century, and in opposition to a political attempt to redefine the Powhatans as "colored" in this century (cf. Rountree 1986: 197-200, 1990: 219-35). The language may no longer be used, but documents such as this one permit its study. This need not be exclusively of academic interest, even, as the Powhatan tribes continue to exist despite all they have been subjected to, and continue to have an interest in their own history.

—Frederic W. Gleach 1999

## Bibliography and Recommended Reading

Aubin, George. 1975. *A Proto-Algonquian Dictionary.* Ottawa: National Museum of Man.

Barbour, Philip L. (ed.). 1969. *The Jamestown Voyages Under the First Charter, 1606-1609.* Cambridge: Hakluyt Society.

Beverley, Robert. 1947. *The History and Present State of Virginia* [1705]. Ed. Louis B. Wright. Chapel Hill: Universityof North Carolina Press.

Bloomfield, Leonard. 1946. Algonquian. In *Linguistic Structures of Native America.* Ed. Cornelius Osgood. Viking Fund Publications in Anthropology, no. 6. New York: Viking Fund.

Feest, Christian. 1990. *The Powhatan Tribes.* New York: Chelsea House.

Geary, James A. 1953. Strachey's Vocabulary of Indian Words Used in Virginia, 1612. In *The Historie of Travell into Virginia Britannia* (1612). Ed. Louis B. Wright and Virginia Freund. London: The Hakluyt Society.

Gerard, William R. 1904. The Tapahanek dialect of Virginia. *American Anthropologist* n.s. 6(2):313-30.

Gleach, Frederic W. 1997. *Powhatan's World and Colonial Virginia: A Conflict of Cultures.* Lincoln: University of Nebraska Press.

Goddard, Ives. 1978. Eastern Algonquian Languages. In *Handbook of North American Indians*, vol. 15, *Northeast*. Ed. Bruce G. Trigger. Washington: Smithsonian Institution Press.

Goddard, Ives (ed.). 1996. *Handbook of North American Indians*, vol 17, *Languages*. Washington: Smithsonian Institution Press.

Harrington, John P. 1955. The Original Strachey Vocabulary of the Virginia Indian Language. *Bureau of American Ethnology Bulletin 157*, Anthropological Papers No. 46. Washington: Government Printing Office.

Hewson, John. 1993. *A Computer-Generated Dictionary of Proto-Algonquian*. Ottawa: Canadian Museum of Civilization.

Jefferson, Thomas. 1955. *Notes on the State of Virginia*. Ed. William Peden. Chapel Hill: University of North Carolina Press.

Michelson, Truman. 1933. The Linguistic Classification of Powhatan. *American Anthropologist* 35(3):549.

Mook, Maurice A. 1943. Virginia Ethnology from an Early Relation. *William and Mary Quarterly*, 2d. ser., 23(2):101-29.

Rountree, Helen C. 1986. Ethnicity among the "Citizen" Indians of Tidewater Virginia, 1800-1930. In *Strategies for Survival: American Indians in the Eastern United States*. Ed. Frank W. Porter III. New York: Greenwood Press.

Rountree, Helen C. 1989. *The Powhatan Indians of Virginia: Their Traditional Culture.* Norman: University of Oklahoma Press.

Rountree, Helen C. 1990. *Pocahontas's People: The Powhatan Indians of Virginia through Four Centuries.* Norman: University of Oklahoma Press.

Siebert, Frank T., Jr. 1975. Resurrecting Virginia Algonquian from the Dead: The Reconstituted and Historical Phonology of Powhatan. In *Studies in Southeastern Indian Languages.* Ed. James M. Crawford. Athens: University of Georgia Press.

Strachey, William. 1849. *The Historie of Travaile into Virginia Britannia.* Ed. R. H. Major. London: The Hakluyt Society.

Strachey, William. 1953. *The Historie of Travell into Virginia Britannia* (1612). Ed. Louis B. Wright and Virginia Freund. London: The Hakluyt Society.

# Excerpt from The Historie of Travaile into Virginia Britannia

The great emperour at this time amongst them, we comondly call Powhatan, for by that name, true yt is, he was made knowne unto us when we arrived in the country first, and so, indeed, he was generally called when he was a yong man, as taking his denomination from the country Powhatan, wherin he was borne, which is above the Falls, as before mentioned, right over aneinst the islands, at the head of our river, and which place, or birth-right of his, he sold, *anno* 1609, about September, unto Captain Francys West, our lord generall's brother, who therefore erected there a fort, calling yt West's Fort, and sate himself down there with one hundred and twenty English; the inhabitants themselves, especially his frontier neighbour prince, call him still Powhatan; his owne people sometimes call him Ottaniack, sometyme Mamanatowick, which last signifies "great king"; but his proper right name, which they salute him with (himself in presence), is Wahunsenacawh.

The greatnes and boundes of whose empire, by reason of his powerfulnes and ambition in his youth, hath larger lymitts then ever had any of his predicessors in former tymes, for he seemes to comaund south and north from the Mangoages and Chawonoaks bordering upon Roanoake, and the Old Virginia, to Tockwogh, a towne pallisadode, standing at the north end of the bay, in forty degrees or thereabouts; south-west to Anoeg (not expressed in the mappe), whose howses are built as ours, ten daies distant from us, from whence those Weroances sent unto him of their comodityes; as Weinock, a servant, in whom Powhatan reposed much trust, would tell our elder planters, and could repeat many wordes of their language he had learned among them in his ymployment thither for his kinge, and whence he often returned, full of presents, to Powhatan, west to Monahassanugh, which stands at the foote of the mountaines; nor-west to the borders of Massawomeck and Bocootawwonough, his enemyes; nor-east and by east to Accohanock, Accowmack, and some other petty nations, lying on the east side of our bay.

He hath divers seates or howses; his chief, when we came into the country, was upon Pamunky River, on the north side or Pembrook side, called Werowocomoco, which, by interpretacion, signifies kinges'-howse; howbeit, not liking to neighbour so neere us, that house being within some fifteen or sixteen miles where he saw we purposed to hold ourselves, and from whence, in six or seven howers, we were able to visit him, he removed, and ever since hath most what kept at a place in the desarts called Orapaks, at the top of the river Chickahamania, betweene Youghtamund and Powhatan. He is a goodly old man, not yet shrincking, though well beaten with many cold and stormye winters, in which he hath bene patient of many necessityes and attempts of his fortune to make his name and famely great. He is supposed to be little lesse than eighty yeares old, I dare not saye how much more; others saye he is of a tall stature and cleane lymbes, of a sad aspect, rownd fatt visaged, with graie haires, but plaine and thin, hanging upon his broad showlders; some few haires upon his chin, and so on his upper lippe: he hath bene a strong and able salvadge, synowye, and of a daring spirit, vigilant, ambitious, subtile to enlarge his dominions: for, but the countryes Powhatan, Arrohatock, Appamatuck, Panunky, Youghtamund, and Mattapamient, which are said to come unto him by inheritance, all the rest of the territories before named and expressed in the mappe, and which are all adjoyning to that river whereon we are seated, they report (as is likewise before remembred) to have been eyther by force subdued unto him, or through feare yeilded: cruell he hath bene, and quarrellous as well with his owne weroances for triffles, and that to strike a terrour and awe into them of his power and condicion, as also with his neighbours in his yonger days, though now delighted in security and pleasure, and therefore stands upon reasonable condicions of peace with all the great and absolute weroances about him, and is likewise more quietly settled amongst his owne.

—William Strachey, 1612

# POWHATAN — ENGLISH

**Aamowk,** *angle.*
**Aayxkehake,** *spade.*
**Abescur,** *a vein.* Bodl. **abescut**.
**Accecow,** *a spark of fire.*
**Accomodemsk,** *turtle.*
**Accongaivwh,** *to bend.*
**Accoondews,** *blue berries of the bigness of grapes, very pleasant.*
**Accopaatamun,** *to feed with a spoon.*
**Accowson,** *to step, to go up.*
**Ackohican,** *to make a dish.*
**Acomtan,** *boat.* Bodl. **aointan**.
**Adamoin,** *to fall.* Bodl. **vdamoin**.
**Adamosū,** *to fall.* Bodl. **vdamosun**.
**Ahcohkinnemun,** *to carry upon one's shoulder.* Bodl. **ahcohkinemun**.
**Ahcoushe,** *to climb a tree.*
**Ahgwur,** *to cover one.*
**Ahkij,** *to hurt, or a thing that hurts me.*
**Ahone,** *God.*
**Ahpewk,** *feathers.*
**Ahqwass,** *a pillow to lay under one's head* (Bodl.)
**Ahqwohhooc,** *dram.*
**Ahshaham,** *lobster.*
**Ahshowcutteis,** *a bird with carnation-colored wings.*
**Ahsmenuns,** *a walnut.* Bodl. **assinenuns**.
**Ahtowvun,** *to make a frame or boat.*
**Ahtur,** *it stinks.*

**Aiossapanijk,** *flying squirrel.*
**Aitowh,** *ball.*
**Akontant,** *playster.*
**Amahoth,** *target.*
**Amaiuwh,** *a great way.*
**Amenacacac,** *seeds.* Bodl. **amenacarac.**
**Amin,** *to bite.*
**Amkonning,** *the blossom of a black cherry deadly poison.* (Bodl.)
**Ammawskin,** *to fall.*
**Ammomū,** *to sow.* Bodl. **amemomu.**
**Amonsoquath,** *bear.*
**Amosens,** *daughter.*
**Ampconomindg,** *to make a spoon.*
**Ampkone,** *frying pan.*
**Amunwhokk,** *target.* Bodl. **amun whoek.**
**Amuwoir,** *to take heed.* Bodl. **amwoir.**
**Anah,** *farewell, or the word at parting.*
**Anansecoon,** *mat made of reeds.* Bodl. **anansacoon.**
**Ananson,** *a mat.*
**Anaskimmins,** *acorn.* Bodl. **anaskimmens.**
**Anaskomens,** *acorns.*
**Anath,** *farewell.*
**Ancagwins,** *pot.*
**Anowwoninr,** *to suck.* Bodl. **anowwonir.**
**Aotawk,** *rat.*
**Apacet,** *to throw away.*
**Apahhammundg,** *to go after.*

**Apahpun**, *a stool to sit upon*. (Bodl.)
**Aparoumenans**, *wheat parched in the fire*.
**Apegwus**, *mouse*.  Bodl. **apegwas**.
**Apetawh poan**, *to toast or broil bread*.
**Apoanocanosutch**, *to make bread*.
**Apokan**, *tobacco pipe*.
**Apome**, *thigh*.
**Apones**, *bread*.
**Apooke**, *tobacco*.
**Apopaqwatecus**, *alone*.  Bodl. **apopagwetecus**.
**Aposon**, *beast in bigness like a pig and in taste alike.* [opossum]  Bodl. **aposoum**.
**Apouscase**, *slowworm*.
**Apowhoh-homins**, *whelps*.  Bodl. **aphohomins**.
**Apowssaw**, *to roast*.
**Appoans**, *bread*.
**Apquammon**, *a show*.
**Aquintayne manggoy**, *great ship*.
**Aquintayne taux**, *little boat, canoe*.
**Aquointan**, *canoe, small boat*.
**Aqwahussun**, *coat of plate*.  Bodl. **agwahvssum**.
**Aqwaskawwans**, *waves of the sea*.  Bodl. **agwaskawwans**.
**Aqwataneik**, *green tree*.  Bodl. **vsqwatanaik**.
**Aramiath south**, *I am sick*.
**Arathkone**, *beast like a fox*.
**Ariqwossac**, *aunts*.  Bodl. **arigwossac**.
**Aroummossouth**, *to be sick*.  Bodl. **arummossouth**.
**Arrahqwotuwh**, *clouds*.  Bodl. **arrahgwotuwh**.

**Arrokoth,** *sky.*
**Asapan,** *hasty pudding.*
**Asasqueth,** *the clay they make pipes of.* Bodl. **assesqueth.**
**Ascahamū,** *to dress or pitch a boat.* Bodl. **ascahamun.**
**Ascamaner,** *to go along.*
**Ascamauk,** *eel.* Bodl. **as camunk.**
**Ascaxasqwus,** *seaweeds.* Bodl. **ascarasqwus.**
**Ascunmewh,** *raw.*
**Aspamū,** *earth.* Bodl. **aspamun.**
**Asqweowan,** *arrow.* Bodl. **asgweowan.**
**Assahampehooke,** *lobster.*
**Assamuwh,** *head of an arrow that is round.*
**Assaovnsawh,** *feathers of an arrow.* Bodl. **assaovncawh.**
**Assentamens,** *pears.* Bodl. **assentammens.**
**Assentewcaiah,** *it shines.* Bodl. **assentucayah.**
**Asseseim,** *wheat plume.* Bodl. **assesseim.**
**Assimnims,** *walnuts.* Bodl. **assinimins.**
**Assimoest,** *fox.*
**Assowpook,** *a box in which they play a certain kind of game.*
**Assunnoineindge,** *walnut tree.* Bodl. **assunnomeindg.**
**Atapahañ,** *a kixe.* [?]
**Atcheisqwansun,** *to lean against.* Bodl. **atcheisgwansvn.**
**Attaanqwassuwk,** *a star.* Bodl. **attaangwassowk.**
**Attagwassanna,** *west.*
**Attasqwas,** *weeds.*
**Attemous,** *dog.*
**Attomois,** *dog.* Bodl. **attomoys.**

# POWHATAN — ENGLISH

**Attowrin**, *civet cat.*

**Aucogwins**, *kettle.* Bodl. **aucagmins**.

**Aucutgaqwassan**, *copper kettle.* Bodl. **aucutgagwassun**.

**Auhtab**, *bow.*

**Auketuttawh**, *fishhook.*

**Aumaumer**, *awake.* Bodl. **aumaumec**.

**Aumboick**, *a thornbark.* (Bodl.)

**Aumpossaish**, *out, or it is plucked out.*

**Aumpsuwk**, *hearing.*

**Aunshecapa**, *afternoon.*

**Auntemdun**, *to beat out with a cudgel.* Bodl. **aunteindum**.

**Aupeis**, *bowstring.*

**Auppes**, *bowstring.*

**Auputchahgwetaw**, *to cleave or stick fast to a thing.* (Bodl.)

**Aussab**, *net.*

**Autowtaoh**, *ear of wheat.*

**Auutsahamun**, *to take up with a spoon.* Bodl. **anutsahamun**.

**Auutus**, *to stink.*

**Awassew**, *to fly.*

**Awrewhmerersk**, *curled hair.* Bodl. **arorewhmerorsk**.


**Bagwanchy basson**, *girdle.*

**Bahtanomun**, *to warm.*

**Bauqweuwh**, *to fly.* Bodl. **paugweuwh**.

**Bmseran apook**, *to fill the pipe with tobacco.* Bodl. **binseran apooke**.

**Bocata oc kok**, *to strike fire.*

**Bocuttaw,** *fire.* Bodl. **bocuttaow.**
**Boketawh,** *fire.* Bodl. **boketawgh.**

**Cacutterewindg kear,** *what is your name?* Bodl. **cacutterewindg keir.**
**Cacutterewindg yowk,** *what is his name?*
**Cacuttewaas yowk,** *what is this, what do you call this?* (Bodl.)
**Cacuttewindg near,** *what is my name?*
**Caivwh,** *I cannot tell.*
**Cakakesqus,** *rushes.*
**Camange,** *tobacco bag.*
**Camatinge,** *six.*
**Camzowan,** *rain.* Bodl. **camrowan.**
**Cante-cante,** *to sing, to dance.*
**Caqwaih,** *what is this, what do you call this?* (Bodl.)
**Catchcahmun mushe,** *to chop wood.*
**Catzahanzamusheis,** *flame.*
**Caumear-ah,** *to come, (being spoken familiarly or hard by).*
**Caumeir,** *to come, (being spoken familiarly or hard by).*
**Caumenaan,** *now lets go together.*
**Caumorowath,** *to come, (being spoken familiarly or hard by).* Bodl. **camerowath.**
**Cauwaih,** *oysters.*
**Cawahcheims,** *small bird or chicken.*
**Cawassow,** *a covering or mantle made of feathers.* Bodl. **cawassuw** = "a covering to lay upon one."

**Cawcawmear**, *to go along.*
**Cawesewh**, *to be like to fall.*
**Cawmdguc**, *bramble, briar.* Bodl. **cawmdgus**.
**Cawqweawans**, *stockings.* Bodl. **cawgweawans**.
**Cawwaivwh**, *bed.*
**Ceumcats**, *a fowl like a teal with a sharp bill like a blackbird.*
**Chakasowe**, *crack.*
**Chamah**, *welcome, or the word of greeting.*
**Chapant**, *shoe.*
**Cheawanta**, *robin red-breast.*
**Checinqwamins**, *a nut like a small acorn, good meat.* Bodl. **chechinquamins**.
**Cheiksew**, *mariner, seaman.*
**Cheipsin**, *land.*
**Cheiscunnemun**, *to wipe one's nose.* (Bodl.)
**Cheisk**, *all.*
**Chesawk**, *rind of a tree like hemp.*
**Cheskchamay**, *all friends.*
**Chessunnaansun**, *to make a mat.*
**Chichiquāmins**, *a kind of grain to eat.*
**Chingissum**, *it is warm or hot weather.*
**Chippsin**, *land, earth.*
**Chmgawwonawk**, *rattle such as they use in their ceremonies, made of a gourd.* Bodl. **chingawwonauk**.
**Chowhwasuw**, *ague.*
**Coan**, *snow.*
**Cohqwaivwh**, *calm.* Bodl. **cohgwaivwh**.

**Coiahqwus**, *gull*. Bodl. **coiahgwus**.
**Commomais**, *you love*. Bodl. **cummomais**.
**Commotins**, *turtle*.
**Commotoouh**, *to steal*. Bodl. **commotooah**.
**Cotappesseaw**, *upset, or a boat to turn keel up*.
**Cowcacunnenuñ**, *to make a frame or boat*.
**Cowichawwotun**, *now lets go together*.
**Cowijhpaantamū**, *to lie together*. Bodl. **cowijhpaantamun**.
**Cowwotaioh**, *summer*.
**Crenepo**, *woman*.
**Cucheneppo**, *woman*.
**Cummeish yoowah**, *give it to him*.
**Cummundgū**, *to cut the hair of a man's head*. Bodl. **cummundgum**.
**Cunnaivwh**, *long*.
**Cunnaqueis**, *to swell*.
**Cunsenagwus**, *an Indian hatchet*.
**Cuppatoan**, *sturgeon*. Bodl. **cuppotoon**.
**Cuppeh**, *yea, yes*.
**Cuppenauk**, *gate*. Bodl. **cuppenawk**.
**Cuppotaw**, *deaf*.
**Curcye neire**, *I am cold*.
**Cursine**, *sister*.
**Cushe**, *to hide or cover from the rain*.
**Cuskessamun**, *to turn the coals*.
**Cuspurn**, *to tie, to make fast*.
**Cussewh kenneaunten mata mochik**, *I understand you a little but not much*. (Bodl.)

**Cussotunnohaans**, *to open anything.* (Bodl.).

**Cutaantaqwapissun**, *a deer crown or of deers' hair dyed red.* (Bodl.)

**Cutchow matowran**, *to burn as if a shake light on anything.* Bodl. **cutchow, matowram**.

**Cutsecammo**, *the cock crows.*

**Cutsotahwooc**, *board.*

**Cutssenepo**, *woman.*

**Cuttack**, *otter.* Bodl. **cuttak**.

**Cuttahamunourcar**, *to make a grave.*

**Cuttaheum meis**, *to look one's head.*

**Cuttaqwocum**, *to pull one down.*

**Cuttassamais**, *beggar.*

**Cuttenamvwhwa**, *polecat.*

**Cuttepacus**, *day.*

**Cutterah**, *to tell.*

**Cutterewh**, *to grow high.*

**Cuttoundg**, *to bark.*

**Cuttoxeen**, *weary.* Bodl. **cuttoreen**.


**Damisac**, *knife.* Bodl. **pamisac**.

**Dawbasonquire**, *warm yourself.*


**Esepannuwh**, *hard.* Bodl. **esepannawh**.

**Eskowwascus**, *sedge.*


**Fatacaumexan**, *sparrow hawk.*

**Gaukenates**, *to dry by fire or otherwise.*
**Geispun**, *to be full.*

**Hamkone**, *ladle.*
**Hatacqwoear**, *hold it aside.*
**Hauquequins**, *a little stone pot.* Bodl. **hauguequins**.
**Hawtoppe**, *bow.*
**Hawtorinkanaske**, *a black fox skin or an overgrown sables'.*
**Howghweyh takon neire**, *I am hungry.* Bodl. **howh weih takon neire**.
**Huskpemmo poketaws**, *to sow wheat.* Bodl. **huskpemmo poketawes**.
**Huspissaan**, *to leap.*
**Husquamun**, *to sew with a needle.* Bodl. **husquamū**.
**Husque**, *by and by, quickly.*
**Husquequenatora**, *now I understand you.* Bodl. **husqueguenatora**.

**Iaheasomaw**, *to light.*
**Iakesan apooke**, *light tobacco.*
**Inspungwaren**, *to wink.* (Bodl.)
**Ioughqueme wath**, *let us go or come away.*
**Ire assuminge**, *go and run quickly.*
**Ireh**, *to go.*
**Ireh cuppeintanaan**, *to go down.* Bodl. **ireh cuppemtanaan**.
**Ireh vscoend**, *to go abroad.*

**Jacuttehwoon**, *to cleanse a pipe.*

**Kaasun**, *village.*
**Kahangoc**, *goose.*
**Kahunge**, *goose.*
**Kameyhan**, *rain.* Bodl. **komeyhon**.
**Kantikantie**, *sing and dance.*
**Kantokan**, *to dance.*
**Kanyough**, *I know not.* Bodl. **kawyough**.
**Kapessemapaangun**, *give me a little piece.*
**Kawkopen quier**, *I drink to you.*
**Kawmdvppaan**, *headache.* Bodl. **kawmclirppaan**.
**Kawwin**, *sleep.*
**Kayquiose**, *boat.*
**Kear**, *you.*
**Kecuttannowas**, *lightning.*
**Keihtascooc**, *snake, adder.*
**Keij**, *out, away, or get you gone.*
**Keis**, *how many.*
**Keiskecamon**, *to kick, to spurn.*
**Kekenohaivwh uspewh**, *not gone up.* Bodl. **kekenohaivmh uspewh**.
**Kekepemgwah**, *smoke.*
**Kekewh**, *alive.*
**Kekitchuchun**, *to tickle someone.* (Bodl.)
**Kekuttun**, *to say.* Bodl. **kecutton**.
**Kemaantuñ**, *to speak softly.*
**Kemotte**, *brother.*

**Kenah**, *I thank you.* Bodl. **kenagh**.
**Kencuttemaum**, *good morrow, or the word of salutation.*
**Keneiwuh**, *sharp.* Bodl. **keneiwoh**.
**Kennehautows**, *I understand well.*
**Kenorockonoren quire**, *come look at my head.* Bodl. **konnockkonoren quire**.
**Kensekit**, *arse.*
**Kequasson**, *a pot to drink in.* Bodl. **keguasson**.
**Keseiceindcher**, *to wash the hand.* Bodl. **keseireindcher**.
**Keseiqwaan**, *to wash the face.* Bodl. **keseigwaan**.
**Keshackaivwh**, *dirt.* Bodl. **kesshackaivwh**.
**Keshawtewh**, *light.*
**Keshemaik pooc**, *the tobacco is naught.*
**Keshowse**, *the sun.* Bodl. **kelhowse**.
**Kesshekissum**, *to laugh.* Bodl. **kesshekisson**.
**Kesshemauc**, *weak.*
**Kessohikear**, *shut the door.* Bodl. **kessahikear**.
**Ketarowksumah**, *to break all in pieces.*
**Ketssetawun**, *to wash anything.*
**Kicke**, *mother.* Bodl. **kick**.
**Kicketen quier**, *speak, tell me.*
**Kijhtoroon**, *a pike.* (Bodl.)
**Kikithamots**, *the wind.* Bodl. **kykeythamots**.
**Kispurracautapus**, *garter.*
**Komeratimiere quier**, *you gave it to me.* (Bodl.)
**Koske**, *ten.*
**Kouppathe**, *yea truly.*
**Kowse**, *father.*

**Kucopen**, *to drink to one.* Bodl. **kakopen**.
**Kuttchawe**, *I burn.*
**Kykeytawe**, *nine.*

**Maangairagwatowh**, *a great hole.* Bodl. **maangairagwatonu**.
**Maangwaoap**, *the girth or leather that girds their middles.* (Bodl.)
**Maangwipacus**, *leaves.*
**Macauqs caunomel**, *a grape's stone or the stone of any plum.* Bodl. **macaugs caunomel**.
**Machacammac**, *a great house.*
**Machenecawwun**, *to lie down to sleep.*
**Machequeo**, *a show.* Bodl. **matchqueo**.
**Macherew**, *enemy.*
**Machess**, *low.*
**Maentchatemayoac**, *gone.*
**Mahawke**, *gourd.*
**Mahcataowh**, *to paint black.* (Bodl.)
**Mahcatawaiuwh**, *black.*
**Mahcatois**, *a coal of fire.*
**Mahcawq**, *a pumpkin.* Bodl. **mahcawg**.
**Mahmaindg-nohaivwh**, *I have none.*
**Mahqwaih**, *a great wind.* Bodl. **mahgwaih**.
**Majawh**, *straight.*
**Makateweygh**, *pearl.* Bodl. **makataweygh**.
**Makique**, *snot.* Bodl. **makigue**.
**Malacommeir**, *I will not give it.*

**Mamantū terracan**, *to play at any game.* Bodl. **mamantu terracaun.**

**Mamarenaretum**, *to wrestle.*

**Mammahe sucqwahum**, *give me some water.* Bodl. **mainmahe sucqwa.**

**Mammaum**, *clouds.* Bodl. **mammau.**

**Mammun**, *to take hold of.*

**Mamoindgakij**, *it hurts me not, it is whole or well.*

**Manaang-gwas**, *butterfly.*

**Mananst**, *little stone.* Bodl. **manansk.**

**Mangeker**, *the height of anything at a good growth.*

**Mangoite**, *great.*

**Maniasc cake**, *to cut rushes.* Bodl. **mamasc cakokesqwus.**

**Mannottaihcaun**, *to make a basket.*

**Manote**, *basket.*

**Mantchoor**, *coat, jerkin, doublet, etc.*

**Maquascawnomell**, *plum stone.* Bodl. **maquascawnomel.**

**Maquiquins**, *small bells.* Bodl. **maquequins.**

**Maraak**, *cedar.*

**Maracah**, *apple.*

**Marahungoc**, *gosling.*

**Marapo**, *enemy.*

**Marrakimmins**, *grapes.*

**Marrapoth quier**, *the wild words they have.* (Bodl.)

**Maskihaan**, *to be melancholy, to be sad.* Bodl. **maskihaon.**

**Maskowhinge**, *parrot.* Bodl. **maskawhinge.**

**Massacamwmdg**, *parrot.*

**Mata-nowwontamen**, *not to hear.*

**Matacawiak,** *pearl.*
**Matacawqweowanneth,** *I have no hose.* Bodl. **matacoawqwrowanneh.**
**Matackesa,** *it is not lighted.*
**Matagvenatoxoth,** *I understand you not.* Bodl. **mataguenatoroth.**
**Matah,** *no, nay.*
**Mataheigh catommoik,** *apron or any kind of dressed leather.* Bodl. **mattaheih, catommoik.**
**Matakennowntorawh,** *I understand not.* Bodl. **matakennowntorowh.**
**Matakuske,** *leaf of a prickle pear.*
**Matamawcasunneh,** *I have no shoes.* Bodl. **matamowcasunneh.**
**Matanamowun,** *not to see.* (Bodl.)
**Mataquiwun,** *red dye.*
**Matassaih,** *napkin, linen.* Bodl. **matassaith.**
**Matassumitohook,** *a small bird of diverse colors.* Bodl. **matassumitohooke.**
**Matassuñ,** *copper.*
**Matavppoannonuwh,** *I have no tobacco.*
**Matavtapawpeak,** *you have no lice.*
**Matawiowijh,** *bachelor.*
**Matchkore,** *skin of a stag.*
**Mattanahayyough,** *I have it not.*
**Mattaquenatorath,** *I understand you not.*
**Mattath,** *no.*
**Mattcheroth quier,** *the wild words they have.* (Bodl.)

**Matush**, *I will not.*
**Maucaqwins**, *bell.* Bodl. **maucaguins**.
**Maucatawatsomeon**, *ear of new wheat.*
**Mauhsaan**, *nettle.*
**Maunomommaon**, *prayer.* Bodl. **maunumommaan**.
**Mawhcasuns**, *shoes.*
**Maxatsno**, *the tongue.* Bodl. **maratsno**.
**Mayanse**, *I have it not.* Bodl. **mayance**.
**Mayis**, *going in a path.* Bodl. **mayn**.
**Mbococotamen**, *to make a hole.* Bodl. **mbocacotamen**.
**Meascoh**, *arms.*
**Meatsun**, *to sup.*
**Mecher**, *to eat.*
**Mechijn**, *ears of a hare or any other beast.*
**Mechocusk**, *I'll eat by and by.*
**Mehkewh**, *beak, bill.*
**Mehtacooc**, *a stalk.*
**Mehteqweins**, *grass.*
**Mehtoan**, *a month.* (Bodl.)
**Meihkeih**, *a sore.*
**Meihkeis**, *wart.*
**Meihsutterask**, *creek.*
**Meihtawk**, *ear of a man.*
**Meihteams**, *a waterfowl in bigness of a duck, finely colored with a copit crown.*
**Meihtinge**, *a hand.*
**Meihtoram**, *post.*
**Meihtucs**, *tree.* Bodl. **meihtus**.

**Meihtussan**, *the spars of a house*. (Bodl.).
**Meihtussuc**, *eat with me*. Bodl. **meihtussur**.
**Meishmicoan chessoyowk**, *give this to the child*. Bodl. **meish miroan chessoyowk**.
**Meishnahmecher**, *give me some meat*.
**Meisquan**, *elbow*.
**Mekouse**, *nails of the fingers and toes*. Bodl. **mekonse**.
**Memmowchicktagwassan**, *to speak aloud*. (Bodl.)
**Memnunnahqus**, *island*. Bodl. **mennunnahgus**.
**Mendabuccah**, *head of a man*.
**Mepit**, *the teeth*.
**Meqwanoc**, *a long feather*.
**Mereengass**, *a shooting glove* (Bodl.).
**Merersc**, *hair of the head*. Bodl. **mexersc**.
**Meroathachessum**, *young boy*. Bodl. **meroathachessam**.
**Mese**, *arm*.
**Meshpataan bocotaoh**, *to fetch some fire*.
**Meskew**, *the nose*. Bodl. **meskewe**.
**Meskott**, *the leg*. Bodl. **mescot**.
**Messeate**, *the foot*.
**Messetonaance**, *beard*. Bodl. **messetonaanse**.
**Messetts**, *feet*. Bodl. **messets**.
**Metacum**, *louse*.
**Metatvwh neckatam**, *all is out*.
**Metawke**, *the ears*.
**Meteingeies**, *the fingers*. (Bodl.)
**Metmge**, *hand*. Bodl. **metinge**.
**Mettone**, *the mouth*.

**Metucs,** *bridge.*
**Metucsmarakimmins,** *bunch of grapes.* Bodl. **metucsmarakimins.**
**Mhnomun,** *to set down anything.* (Bodl.)
**Minchin,** *you eat.* Bodl. **mittchin.**
**Minchin quire,** *you eat.* Bodl. **minchin quier.**
**Mintabukhan,** *the head.* Bodl. **mintabukham.**
**Miske,** *here.*
**Missanek,** *squirrel.*
**Mocosijt,** *a woman's privates.* Bodl. **mucosiit.**
**Mohwhaiok,** *moth.*
**Moich,** *turd.*
**Moieh,** *filthy.*
**Moincaminge,** *dead leaves.*
**Moiowat,** *filthy.* Bodl. **moiowatt.**
**Momonsacqweo,** *bear.* Bodl. **monnonsacqueo.**
**Momuscken,** *a mole in the ground.*
**Monahamshaw,** *bird like a lapwing, color gray, which uses the water.*
**Monanaw,** *turkey.*
**Monascunnemū,** *to cleanse the ground and make it fit for seed.* Bodl. **monascunnemun.**
**Moninaw,** *the cock crows.* Bodl. **moninawcutsecamo.**
**Monohacan,** *sword.*
**Monowhauk,** *sword.* Bodl. **monowhaake.**
**Monynawgh,** *turkey.* Bodl. **moninagh.**
**Moowchick,** *a great deal.*
**Moroke,** *cedar.*

**Mouhwacus**, *marten*.
**Moundg**, *to cut the hair of a man's head*.
**Mounshaqwatuwh**, *heaven*. Bodl. **mounshagwatowh**.
**Moussomko**, *squirrel*.
**Mowchesoh**, *a fly*.
**Mowcheson**, *a fly*.
**Mowhkohan**, *fishhook*.
**Mowsah**, *maggot, little worm*.
**Muckatahone**, *the arm*.
**Mummascushenepo**, *I have been asleep*. Bodl. **mummacushenepaw**.
**Mundgtacan**, *shears*. Bodl. **moundgtacan**.
**Muscaivwh**, *glorious, smooth, beautiful*.
**Muscaussum**, *bright or plain all over*.
**Mushawwacat**, *I am lither or lazier*.
**Musheis-in-ourowh**, *wood all along*. (Bodl.)
**Muskaivwh**, *a flower of a fine thing*. (Bodl.)
**Muskan**, *the forehead*.
**Muskefkimmins**, *strawberries*.
**Muskeis**, *wood*. Bodl. **musheis**.
**Musken**, *to run*. Bodl. **musket**.
**Muskiendguk**, *the eye*.
**Muskiendues**, *the eyes*. Bodl. **muskiendgues**.
**Muskins**, *the eyes*. Bodl. **musknis**.
**Muskimmins**, *a mulberry*. Bodl. **muskimnis**.
**Mussaangegwah**, *maneaters*.
**Mussane**, *a beast so called*.
**Mussaran**, *town*.

**Mussetaqwaioh**, *circle*. Bodl. **mussetagwaioh**.
**Mussataquopur**, *to sit further*. (Bodl.)
**Mussowuxuc**, *a ship*. Bodl. **mussawuruc**.
**Mutsun**, *milk*. Bodl. **mutson**.
**Muttaqwohoons**, *to stop or put in a stopple*.
**Muttassapec**, *cobweb*. Bodl. **nuttassapec**.
**Mutusk**, *a woman's privates*.

**Naantam**, *wolf*.
**Naantuc-ah**, *to come again, we will come again*.
**Naantucah-necut**, *only one*.
**Nacowns**, *net*. Bodl. **nacowas**.
**Nahapuc**, *to dwell*. Bodl. **nahapur**.
**Nahayhough**, *I have it*.
**Namaske**, *fish*.
**Nameche**, *fish*.
**Nammais**, *fish*.
**Nanamachauwh**, *the king's name of Roanake*.
**Natapahan**, *kixe*.
**Nawhpomind**, *to lay down a thing*.
**Nawpin**, *to sit down*.
**Nawwiowashim**, *to carry a thing up and down*. Bodl. **nowwicwashim**.
**Near**, *I*.
**Nearnowwan**, *I have been*.
**Necakessuttun**, *to take one prisoner*. Bodl. **necakessutton**.
**Necantuwh**, *to pull it out*. Bodl. **necantough**.
**Nechañ**, *child*.

**Mouhwacus**, *marten.*
**Moundg**, *to cut the hair of a man's head.*
**Mounshaqwatuwh**, *heaven.* Bodl. **mounshagwatowh**.
**Moussomko**, *squirrel.*
**Mowchesoh**, *a fly.*
**Mowcheson**, *a fly.*
**Mowhkohan**, *fishhook.*
**Mowsah**, *maggot, little worm.*
**Muckatahone**, *the arm.*
**Mummascushenepo**, *I have been asleep.* Bodl. **mummacushenepaw**.
**Mundgtacan**, *shears.* Bodl. **moundgtacan**.
**Muscaivwh**, *glorious, smooth, beautiful.*
**Muscaussum**, *bright or plain all over.*
**Mushawwacat**, *I am lither or lazier.*
**Musheis-in-ourowh**, *wood all along.* (Bodl.)
**Muskaivwh**, *a flower of a fine thing.* (Bodl.)
**Muskan**, *the forehead.*
**Muskefkimmins**, *strawberries.*
**Muskeis**, *wood.* Bodl. **musheis**.
**Musken**, *to run.* Bodl. **musket**.
**Muskiendguk**, *the eye.*
**Muskiendues**, *the eyes.* Bodl. **muskiendgues**.
**Muskins**, *the eyes.* Bodl. **musknis**.
**Muskimmins**, *a mulberry.* Bodl. **muskimnis**.
**Mussaangegwah**, *maneaters.*
**Mussane**, *a beast so called.*
**Mussaran**, *town.*

**Mussetaqwaioh,** *circle.* Bodl. **mussetagwaioh.**
**Mussataquopur,** *to sit further.* (Bodl.)
**Mussowuxuc,** *a ship.* Bodl. **mussawuruc.**
**Mutsun,** *milk.* Bodl. **mutson.**
**Muttaqwohoons,** *to stop or put in a stopple.*
**Muttassapec,** *cobweb.* Bodl. **nuttassapec.**
**Mutusk,** *a woman's privates.*

**Naantam,** *wolf.*
**Naantuc-ah,** *to come again, we will come again.*
**Naantucah-necut,** *only one.*
**Nacowns,** *net.* Bodl. **nacowas.**
**Nahapuc,** *to dwell.* Bodl. **nahapur.**
**Nahayhough,** *I have it.*
**Namaske,** *fish.*
**Nameche,** *fish.*
**Nammais,** *fish.*
**Nanamachauwh,** *the king's name of Roanake.*
**Natapahan,** *kixe.*
**Nawhpomind,** *to lay down a thing.*
**Nawpin,** *to sit down.*
**Nawwiowashim,** *to carry a thing up and down.* Bodl. **nowwicwashim.**
**Near,** *I.*
**Nearnowwan,** *I have been.*
**Necakessuttun,** *to take one prisoner.* Bodl. **necakessutton.**
**Necantuwh,** *to pull it out.* Bodl. **necantough.**
**Nechañ,** *child.*

**Nechaun,** *child.*
**Necoondamen,** *it is good meat.*
**Necqurissar,** *I dare not.* Bodl. **necgwussaw.**
**Necussagwns,** *to carry a thing between two.*
**Necutchucskuw,** *to scrub one's head.* Bodl. **necutchuckskuw.**
**Negeisp,** *I am full.*
**Nehapper,** *sit down.*
**Nehapper kupper,** *sit further.*
**Nehpaangunnū,** *blind.* Bodl. **nehpaangvnnu.**
**Nehsaakah,** *reed.*
**Neighsawhor,** *to come down.*
**Neighseum,** *to cry.*
**Neihpyahraiab,** *I will come tomorrow.* (Bodl.)
**Neihpunsannvwh,** *to make blunt.*
**Neihsacan,** *a weir to take fish.*
**Neimbat,** *enough.*
**Neir,** *myself.* Bodl. **neire.**
**Neire,** *I am sick.*
**Nek,** *mother.* Bodl. **neck.**
**Nekereinskeps,** *ring.*
**Nekut,** *one.*
**Nemat,** *brother.*
**Nembobatsoho,** *to miss the hole.* Bodl. **nembabatsoho.**
**Nepassingwahoon,** *to strike.* Bodl. **nepassingwahcon.**
**Nepaun,** *to sleep.*
**Nepausche,** *sun.* Bodl. **nepaushe.**
**Nepawironowh,** *lame.* Bodl. **nepamironowh.**

**Nepensun**, *dust.*
**Nepkehanaan**, *to pinch.* Bodl. **nepokehanaan**.
**Nepocuttokeau**, *a wound.*
**Nepogwaanshepissun**, *a girdle.* (Bodl.)
**Nepokeunnamū**, *to soak bread.* Bodl. **nepokevnnamun**.
**Nepomotamen**, *to shoot.* Bodl. **nepomatamen**.
**Nepopawinin**, *to go before.* Bodl. **nepopawmin**.
**Nepotatamen**, *to blow anything.*
**Nepowwer**, *naked.*
**Neppe**, *wet.*
**Nepunche neir**, *I am dead.* Bodl. **nepuncke neire**.
**Neputte**, *the teeth.*
**Nequtahke**, *I dare not.* Bodl. **negutahke**.
**Neqwaxulloundwun**, *to snort.* Bodl. **nequarattoundmun**.
**Netab**, *friend, also the principal word of kindness; I am your friend, I am at your command; welcome, or the word of greeting.* Bodl. **netah**.
**Netacoon**, *a great way.*
**Netap**, *my dear friend.*
**Netapewh**, *I am your friend, I am at your command.*
**Nethkeon**, *the nose.*
**Netshetsunh**, *the soul or vital breath of man.*
**Nettencrianges**, *to be faint.*
**Netuspus**, *to leap as men leap in dancing or otherwise..*
**Neusakaqwan**, *to make a fire.* Bodl. **neusakagwan**.
**Nim**, *aye, yea.*
**Nimatewh**, *man.*
**Nindgapamutla mecreentecoh**, *a king of the head.*

[crown?]
**Nindgvttecohcapar**, *to keel.* (Bodl.)
**Ninge**, *two.*
**Ningepoke**, *twenty.*
**Nisake**, *cane.*
**Nissakan**, *reed.*
**Nmtawooc**, *match.* Bodl. **nintawook**.
**Nocmchamino boketaw**, *mend up the fire.* Bodl. **noringeamind baketaw**.
**Noewanathsoun**, *I have forgotten.*
**Nohaivwh**, *to have.* Bodl. **nohainwh**.
**Noiatewk**, *hungry.*
**Nonattewh**, *faun.* Bodl. **monattecoh**.
**Nonssamats**, *cold.*
**Nooueshetun**, *to beat out with a cudgel.* Bodl. **nooueshetum**.
**Noraughtoan**, *put on your hat.*
**Noumpqwaam**, *porridge, broth.* Bodl. **noumpgwaam**.
**Noungasse**, *wife.* Bodl. **noungass**.
**Noungat**, *to do.*
**Nousomon**, *below.* Bodl. **nousvmon**.
**Nousough**, *three.* Bodl. **nussaugh**.
**Nouwmais**, *I love you.*
**Nowiowijh wiowah**, *married man.*
**Nowqweitut**, *the ring finger.* Bodl. **nomgweitut**.
**Nows**, *father.*
**Nowwanus**, *lost.*
**Nowwuntamen**, *to hear.*

**Nuckaandgum,** *sister.*
**Numerathguran pocoon,** *to paint red.* (Bodl.)
**Numerothequier,** *your companion.*
**Numma,** *will you go home.*
**Nummacha,** *to go home, I will go home.* Bodl. **cunnacha.**
**Nummagwais,** *the pox.* Bodl. **nummanemennaus.**
**Nummamuntam,** *to be faint.*
**Nummaskatamen,** *I care not for it.*
**Nummatchqwran,** *to paint black.* (Bodl.)
**Nummavmon,** *to pull.*
**Nummawh,** *to weep.*
**Nummecaxuttenax,** *fight at fisticuffs.* Bodl. **nummecaxuttenar.**
**Nummechijn,** *I will eat.*
**Nummeisutteidg,** *the little finger.*
**Nummeisutteingwah,** *the fore finger.*
**Nummeraantaan,** *to strew or cast.* (Bodl.)
**Nummeramin,** *to smell.* Bodl. **numeramin.**
**Nummonnemenndus,** *to pluck up.*
**Nummundgū,** *to cut the hair of a man's head.* Bodl. **nummundgum.**
**Numpenamun,** *let me see it.*
**Nuppawē,** *sleep.*
**Nus,** *three.*
**Nuscahsaiyam,** *tawny* (Bodl.)
**Nuscawes,** *eight.* Bodl. **nuschawes.**
**Nusqwoik,** *the neck of anything.*
**Nussaandg,** *elder.*

**Nussacum,** *to bite.* Bodl. **nussacom.**
**Nusseseqwus,** *to whet.* Bodl. **nussesseqwus.**
**Nusshaih,** *lips.*
**Nussuccum,** *to cough.*
**Nuswohcassannack,** *three hundred.* (Bodl.)
**Nutsseqwacup,** *I will drink no more.* Bodl. **nutssegwacup.**
**Nuttacoondah,** *playster.*
**Nuttahcaam,** *deep over the head.*
**Nuttaqwon,** *a flea.*
**Nuttaspin,** *to sow wheat.*
**Nuttawwuttemdg,** *the long finger.*
**Nuwamatamen,** *I must keep it, I love it.*
**Nuwweisqwaput,** *to wrap, to wind up.*


**Ockquetath,** *tassel of a goshawk*
**Ockquins,** *a watchet-colored bird.*
**Ohawas,** *crow.*
**Ohcawooc,** *a well.*
**Ohorinne,** *crooked.* Bodl. **ohhorime.**
**Ohshaangumiemuns,** *shells.* Bodl. **ohshaangannemuns.**
**Ohtamocan,** *barrel.*
**Ohtindge,** *claw of a crab.*
**Oiacpijann,** *to come again, we will come again.*
**Oiawh,** *the lean of any flesh.*
**Okinsher,** *the bob of the gynny wheat without corn.*
**Okisher,** *the bob of the gynny wheat without corn.*
**Oktamocan,** *can or any such thing to drink in.*
**Onascandamen,** *to catch in the mouth as dogs do.*

**Onxe,** *fox.*
**Ootun,** *cheese or any curded matter made of milk.*
**Opaivwh,** *white.*
**Opassontamen,** *to catch in the mouth as dogs do.*
**Opomens,** *chestnuts.*
**Opommins,** *chestnuts.*
**Opotenaiok,** *eagle.* Bodl. **opatenaiok.**
**Opoteyough,** *the pipe is stopped.* Bodl. **opoteyawh.**
**Opykerough,** *a brant, a fowl like a goose.*
**Oreih,** *ice.*
**Oremgeis,** *feet of a hawk.* Bodl. **oreingeis.**
**Oronocah,** *a garden or plot of ground to sow corn.* Bodl. **oronacah.**
**Osaih,** *blew.*
**Osaioh,** *yesterday.* Bodl. **osayoh.**
**Osakescai,** *cockle.*
**Osanintak,** *candle or gummy stick which will keep light.* Bodl. **osamintak.**
**Osasianticus,** *divedapper bird.*
**Osasquus,** *muskrat.* Bodl. **osasquws.**
**Osawas,** *brass.*
**Oskeitch,** *above.*
**Ospanno,** *turkey cock.*
**Ossantamens,** *peas.*
**Otakeisheheis,** *guts.*
**Otassantamens,** *peas.* Bodl. **ottassantamens.**
**Otassapnar,** *to call.* Bodl. **otassapiiar.**
**Otassotagwopur,** *to sit nearer.* Bodl. **otassotaqwopur.**

**Otaus,** *breast of a woman.*
**Otawiaac bocataw,** *the fire is out.* Bodl. **otawiaac bocotow**.
**Oteincas,** *glove.*
**Oteingas,** *glove.*
**Oteyquenimin,** *to tear or rend anything.*
**Otsetuns,** *to grow high.*
**Ottanueis,** *train of a bird.* Bodl. **otanneis**.
**Ottawm,** *earth.*
**Ough,** *it is well.*
**Oughrath,** *far off.*
**Oughtamangoyth,** *tobacco bag.*
**Ouhopunnawk,** *a ground nut.*
**Ouhshawkowh,** *a codfish.* (Bodl.)
**Ourcar,** *grave.*
**Ourcrewh,** *purple.*
**Ouronnemunpeta cawwin,** *to make a bed.* (Bodl.)
**Oussawack,** *yellow.*
**Outacan,** *a dish.*
**Owanough,** *who has this.*
**Owaugh,** *egg.*

**Paaksetower,** *to bring into the boat.*
**Paangun,** *a little piece.*
**Paatch nah rungan vdamushcan,** *give me some butter or fat to spread on my bread.* Bodl. **paatchnati rungan vdamuscan**.
**Paatch-ah,** *to give.*

**Paatchkiscaw,** *bald.*

**Paaugahtamuns,** *hazelnut.*

**Pachimoina,** *landsmen (with* amantac *so called because they laboured at sea).* (Bodl.)

**Pacus,** *chest.*

**Pacussac-an,** *a gun or piece.*

**Pahcunnaioh,** *dark.*

**Pahgwurraow,** *sparks that glitter.* (Bodl.)

**Pahquarra,** *a spark of fire.* Bodl. **pahqwarra.**

**Paiamasuw,** *entombing.* Bodl. **paiamasum.**

**Pamahsaivwh,** *the world.* Bodl. **pamahsaivmh.**

**Pamyauk,** *gourd.* Bodl. **pamyack.**

**Paougwnssenttawh,** *to be dry or thirsty.* Bodl. **paougwussenttawh.**

**Papasowh,** *morning, sunrise.*

**Paqwachowng,** *the falls at the upper end of the king's river.* Bodl. **paquachowng.**

**Paqwantawun,** *leather that covers their hips and privates.* Bodl. **pagwantawun.**

**Paseme vppooke,** *give me some tobacco.* Bodl. **paseme vppook.**

**Pasemeh,** *to give.*

**Paskamath,** *mulberries.*

**Paskasew,** *a crack or cracked.*

**Paskeaw,** *to break by striking.*

**Paskorath,** *the gold sparks in the sand.*

**Paspasaat vscantewh,** *the morning is fair.* Bodl. **paspasat vscantewh.**

**Paspeen**, *to go.*
**Paspene**, *to walk about.*
**Pasquehamon**, *to eat.*
**Pasqwuxxaws**, *to wind about.* Bodl. **pasqwurraws**.
**Passagwear**, *to rise up.* Bodl. **passaquear**.
**Passahicaan**, *to clap one's hands.*
**Patewh**, *nearby or next hand.*
**Patow**, *to bring again.*
**Pattihquapisson**, *hat.*
**Paukauns**, *a walnut.* Bodl. **paucauns**.
**Pawpawmear**, *to walk.*
**Pawpecoon**, *to play on a pipe.* (Bodl.)
**Peache**, *fetch, bring.*
**Peccatoas**, *beans.* Bodl. **peccataas**.
**Peihtaoh**, *froth, scum.* Bodl. **peihtach**.
**Peinder**, *to put it in.*
**Peintiker**, *to come in.*
**Peketawes**, *beans.*
**Pemanataon**, *cord or small line, thread.*
**Pemucqweraneind**, *twined thread.* Bodl. **pemuckqweraneind**.
**Pemuntnaw**, *rope, cord.*
**Penim**, *noise of a piece, fall of a tree.*
**Penimathatoan**, *thread.*
**Penninaugh**, *rope.* Bodl. **peminah**.
**Penonge**, *jeron stone.* Bodl. **penouge**.
**Penumun**, *to unclose hands.*
**Perervimuw**, *angry.* Bodl. **perervinnow**.

43

**Perew,** *to be broken or cracked.*
**Perewh,** *naught broken or cracked.* (Bodl.)
**Perrmgqwak,** *to look asquint.* Bodl. **permgwah.**
**Petacawin,** *bed.*
**Petawin,** *ground.* Bodl. **pttawin.**
**Pettackqueth,** *thunder.* Bodl. **petacqueth.**
**Peyeugh,** *returning.*
**Peymmatā,** *thread.*
**Pichamnis,** *an excellent plum.*
**Pickewh,** *the gum that issueth out of a certain tree called the Virginian maple.*
**Pickutts,** *the gum we hold balsam.* Bodl. **pickuts.**
**Pijah,** *to come, being spoken afar off to one.*
**Pijahtamaon,** *to come to prayer.*
**Pijarah,** *to come, being spoken afar off to one.*
**Pijarowah,** *to come, being spoken afar off to one.*
**Pijautch,** *to come again, we will come again.*
**Piscoend,** *duck.*
**Pisquaon,** *duck.*
**Poawamindg,** *oak tree.*
**Poawnncindg,** *oak tree.*
**Pocohaac,** *an awl pin or needle, pin, pestle; the privates of a man.* Bodl. **pocohaac, pohcohaac.**
**Pocohack,** *a bodkin or awl.*
**Pocohiquara,** *milk made of walnuts.* Bodl. **powhigwara.**
**Pocuttawes,** *wheat.* Bodl. **powttoas.**
**Pocututauha,** *husk of their wheat.* Bodl. **pocuntavhea.**
**Poenguwh,** *gnat.* Bodl. **poengwus.**

**Pohcoons,** *red dye.*
**Pohcuwtoah,** *gynny wheat.*
**Poheewh,** *bottle.* Bodl. **paheewh**.
**Pohkevwh,** *otter, or rather a beaver.* Bodl. **pohkeuwh**.
**Poket,** *a fart.*
**Poketawes,** *wheat.*
**Pokeyough,** *to dive underwater.*
**Pokin,** *to dive underwater.* Bodl. **pokin bokeyough**.
**Pokontats,** *girdle.* Bodl. **pocontath**.
**Pokoranse,** *mineral stone.* Bodl. **pokorance**.
**Pokosack,** *gun.* Bodl. **pocosack**.
**Pomahaum,** *snail.*
**Pomevwh,** *woman with child.* Bodl. **powevwh**.
**Pomotawh,** *hill, mountain.*
**Ponomawus,** *widgeon.* Bodl. **ponomaws**.
**Poohkewh,** *to dive.*
**Poomp arrathqwatuwh,** *the elements.*
**Popogwussur,** *hell.*
**Porance,** *five.* Bodl. **parance**.
**Porasap,** *bag.*
**Poshenaan,** *to flee.* Bodl. **pashenaan**.
**Potawaugh,** *porpoise.* Bodl. **patawoc**.
**Potopotawh tawh,** *to boil up.*
**Potterakai,** *it hurts me not, it is whole or well.* Bodl. **potteracai**.
**Poughkone,** *red paint, red dye.* Bodl. **poughcone**.
**Powtowhone boketan,** *blow the fire with your mouth.* Bodl. **powtowhone boketawe**.

**Punguy,** *ashes.* Bodl. **pugguy.**
**Pungwe,** *ashes.*
**Punsaos,** *autumn, the fall of the leaf.*
**Puppaannoh,** *winter.* Bodl. **puppoan noh.**
**Puppoqwahauns,** *to swim as a piece of wood or feather on the water.* Bodl. **puppaqwahauns.**
**Pushenims,** *a plum is very delicious when it is ripe.*
**Pussagwuñ,** *clay.*
**Pussaqwembun,** *rose.* Bodl. **pussaqweinbun.**
**Pussaqwembunameindg,** *rose tree.* (Bodl.)
**Pussaqwunnenidg,** *to put off.* Bodl. **pussaqwonneindg.**
**Pussepussactawas,** *to melt.* Bodl. **pussepussactawos.**
**Puttaiqwapisson,** *cap, hat.*
**Puttawus,** *a covering or mantle made of feathers.* (Bodl.)
**Puttohiqwosur,** *to put on.*

**Quantamum,** *to swallow.* Bodl. **quantamū.**
**Que quoy,** *what is this?*
**Que quoy ternis quire,** *what is your name?*
**Qwananats,** *wood pigeon.*
**Qwangatarask,** *owl.*
**Qwannacut,** *rainbow.* Bodl. **qwannacut.**
**Qwatshacumhcaan,** *to pour out water.* Bodl. **qwatshacuwhcaan.**
**Qweisqwesun,** *to whistle.* Bodl. **qweisgwesun.**
**Qwunnumsc,** *braser.* Bodl. **qwunnumse.**
**Qwunsewh,** *sunset.*

**Racawh**, *sand.*
**Rahsawans**, *leather stripes or strings.*
**Rahtaws**, *lamprey.*
**Raiab**, *tomorrow.*
**Raieawk**, *day.* Bodl. **raioawk**.
**Rapantā**, *venison.*
**Raputtak**, *head of an arrow.*
**Raqwassewhmushe**, *to fall down from a tree.*
**Raragwunnemun**, *to open anything.* (Bodl.).
**Rarascaū**, *air.* Bodl. **rarascaum**.
**Rarenaw**, *chain.*
**Rasannear**, *to run.*
**Rassawans**, *jags of the savages' habit.*
**Rassewocatuwh**, *a grain or croty.* (Bodl.)
**Rassicokear**, *to open the door.*
**Rassoum**, *wind.* Bodl. **rossoun**.
**Rassunnemum**, *to take off.*
**Rawerunnuwh**, *old man.* Bodl. **ramerumuwh**.
**Rawottonemd**, *God.*
**Rawwaiend**, *none.* Bodl. **rawwanud**.
**Reconack**, *tobacco bag.* Bodl. **reconacke**.
**Reihcahahcoik**, *overcast or hidden under a cloud.*
**Reihcawh**, *night.*
**Reihcoan**, *comb.* Bodl. **reihcoun**.
**Rekasque**, *knife.*
**Riapoke**, *the devil; tomorrow.*
**Rickahone**, *comb.*
**Rickewh**, *to divide a thing in half.*

**Riokosick,** *the devil.* Bodl. **riakosicke.**
**Rocoyhook,** *otter.* Bodl. **rokayhook.**
**Rokohamin,** *parched corn ground small.*
**Romuttun,** *hill, small mount.* Bodl. **romutton.**
**Rookewh coan,** *it snows.*
**Rouhcat,** *meal and flour.*
**Rowcar appons,** *piece of bread.* Bodl. **rowrooc appones.**
**Rowhqwawh,** *sheldrake.* Bodl. **rowhgwawh.**
**Rowhsunnvwh,** *the small wind.*
**Rowksewh,** *meal and flour.*
**Rummasvwendg,** *a piece of a pot or potsherd.*
**Rummotaihwh,** *wide or great.* (Bodl.)
**Rungâ,** *all kinds of suet.* Bodl. **rungan.**

**Saccasac,** *to lie with a woman.* Bodl. **saccasak.**
**Sakahocan,** *to write.*
**Sakahooke,** *the clear stones we gather.*
**Sansaqivawwh,** *not to bend.* Bodl. **sansagwaivwh.**
**Sassacomuwah,** *snake, adder.*
**Sawwone,** *salt.*
**Secon,** *to spit.*
**Secqwahan,** *water.*
**Seiscatvwh,** *ebbing water.*
**Sekehekonaugh,** *to write.*
**Shacahocan,** *stone.*
**Shekijn,** *to piss.*
**Socaquinchenimum,** *to make a fire.* Bodl. **socaqwinchenimom.**

**Suckimma**, *new moon.*
**Suckquohana**, *water.* Bodl. **suckquahan**.
**Suttecahamun**, *to knock or beat a thing with a hammer.* (Bodl.)
**Suttekepacatvwh**, *the Spring.* (Bodl.)

**Taangoqwaÿk**, *behind.* Bodl. **tanagogwaiik**.
**Taccahacan**, *hatchet.*
**Taccaho appoans**, *bread made of a woat.* [woat = oat? wheat?] Bodl. **taccahoappouns**.
**Taccahooc**, *block, mortar.* Bodl. **taccahoac**.
**Tackqwaisuw**, *short.* Bodl. **tacqwaisuw**.
**Tacqwacat**, *frost.*
**Tah**, *no, nay.*
**Tahmocassewh**, *he has not or none.*
**Tamahaac**, *hatchet.*
**Tammuscamauwh**, *flowing water.* Bodl. **tammuscamcuwh**.
**Tamohake**, *hatchet.*
**Tamokin**, *to swim.*
**Tanaowaam**, *where have you been?* Bodl. **tannowaam**.
**Tangasuw**, *of a little height.*
**Tangeqwath**, *fur like a sable's.* Bodl. **tangeguath**.
**Tanggo**, *let me see it.*
**Tangoa**, *give it to me or let me see it.*
**Tanoo chunck**, *when.* Bodl. **tannoo chink**.
**Tanx**, *small, little.* Bodl. **tanre**.
**Tapaantaminais**, *chain of copper with long links.*

**Tapacoh,** *night.* Bodl. **tapocoh.**
**Tashoac,** *all is out.*
**Tatacaunshewah,** *grasshopper.*
**Tatamaho,** *garfish.*
**Tatumsew,** *a crack or cracked.*
**Tauosin,** *stool.*
**Taux,** *a little.*
**Tawatuttener,** *to yawn, to gape.*
**Tawhs,** *no more.*
**Tawhtagwountamen,** *to chew.*
**Tchijmaoc,** *to row.* Bodl. **tchiimaac.**
**Tenuecatower,** *to open the door.*
**Thaigwenvmmeraan,** *I give it to you gratis.* Bodl. **thacgwenvmmeraun.**
**Thepahcoon,** *the stalk of gynny or Virginia wheat.* (Bodl.)
**Tohtummocunnum,** *gust, hurricane.*
**Tooskean,** *to swim.*
**Towacqwoins,** *pigeon.* Bodl. **towacgwoins.**
**Towaughe,** *crome.* [crumb?]
**Towawh,** *strong.* Bodl. **towaugh.**
**Tsaqwomoi,** *deep to the middle.*
**Tsehqwun,** *to spit.* (Bodl.)
**Tsekehica,** *to sweep.*
**Tsemahcaug,** *the flower of the apple maraccih.*
**Tsemaosay,** *a sail.*
**Tsenahcommacah,** *Virginia.*
**Tsepaantamen,** *to kiss.*
**Tsepaih,** *dead.*

**Tsetewh**, *to dry by fire or otherwise.*
**Tshecomah**, *a mussel shell.*
**Tshehaoah**, *flax.*
**Tshehip**, *bird.*
**Tshekehicawwuns**, *broom.* Bodl. **tshekehicawwons**.
**Tshemacans**, *oar.*
**Tshepoijn**, *ladle.* Bodl. **thepoyn**.
**Tshetcheindg**, *bird.* Bodl. **tshetchenidg**.
**Tshoegetewh**, *a fowl in likeness of a [?] footed with a sharp beak.* (Bodl.)
**Tumpseis**, *old woman.*
**Tussan**, *a seat in a boat or a bench.*
**Tuttascuc**, *crab.* Bodl. **tuttascuk**.
**Tuttascwh**, *torn, rent.* Bodl. **tuttasewh**.
**Tuwcuppewk**, *sea turtle.* Bodl. **towcuppewk**.

**Uttocais**, *leather.*

**Vannatassun**, *to stand.*
**Vaugh**, *word of wonder.*
**Vcsapess**, *boy.*
**Vdansqwapissun**, *to knot up hair they tie upon their heads.* Bodl. **vdansgwapissun**.
**Vdapungwaren**, *to open one's eyes.*
**Vdasemeodaan**, *to go softly.* Bodl. **vdasemoodaan**.
**Vdeishcawunvppocan**, *the pipe is broken.* (Bodl.)
**Vdeistahamū**, *to break by striking.*
**Vdesinamun**, *to break with one's fingers.* Bodl. **vdesinamum**.

**Vdespunnemun,** *to lift up.*
**Vebowchass,** *to sweat.* Bodl. **vebowhass.**
**Vegwantaak,** *the throat.*
**Vepacaman,** *to strike with a sword.*
**Veroanee,** *king, great man.*
**Vespessemaanpooc,** *to take tobacco.* Bodl. **nepesseanpooc.**
**Vgaucopessum,** *I would drink.*
**Vhpooc,** *tobacco.*
**Vhpoocan,** *tobacco pipe.*
**Vimawh,** *tomorrow.* Bodl. **vnnawh.**
**Vketeqwaivtteindg,** *the thumb.* Bodl. **vketeqwaivtteindg.**
**Vmdguppauk,** *thunder.*
**Vmeqwussum,** *scab.*
**Vmpsemen apook,** *drink, tobacco.* Bodl. **vmpsemen apooke.**
**Vmpsquoth,** *moon.*
**Vnamun,** *to waken.*
**Vnapootain,** *hungry.*
**Vnchgucheis caumelmushe,** *to break a stick.* (Bodl.)
**Vndoth,** *take it.*
**Vnechacuskonahsa,** *I hurt my leg.* (Bodl.)
**Vnechikutchikussa,** *itch.* Bodl. **vnethicvtchikussa.**
**Vnecussopisson,** *to scratch .*
**Vnegapamutta mennetatakij,** *it hurts my legs, or my legs ache.*
**Vneghiawmdupmeputs,** *a king of the teeth.* [crown?] Bodl. **vneghiawindupineputs.**

**Vnekishemū,** *to cut.* Bodl. **vnekishemun.**
**Vnepasknoterahbon,** *to flip with one's finger.* (Bodl.)
**Vnepawahumā,** *a brush.* Bodl. **vnepawahumma.**
**Vneshawocanassup,** *hot weather.*
**Vnetagwushomon,** *blew beads.* Bodl. **vnetagwushowon.**
**Vnetawvnnū,** *to bruise anything small.* Bodl. **vnetawvnnum.**
**Vntowh,** *take it.* Bodl. **vntough.**
**Vpococaheih,** *I must put tobacco in it.* Bodl. **vpacocaheih.**
**Vppeinsaman,** *glue or gum that fasteneth on their arrow heads.*
**Vppocano,** *a tobacco pipe.* (Bodl.)
**Vppocanomowr,** *the pipe is foul.* (Bodl.)
**Vppoo-chappoc,** *tobacco root.*
**Vppoushun mushower,** *the ships go home.* Bodl. **vpponshun mushowr.**
**Vsasarouhketahamū,** *to knock upon one's finger it being pricked.* (Bodl.)
**Vsasqwork,** *pearl mussel shells.* Bodl. **vsasgwoik.**
**Vscaentur,** *the face.*
**Vscannewh,** *not ripe.*
**Vscomtain,** *to go in.* Bodl. **vscomtain.**
**Vscook,** *a fine or small thread.*
**Vscound,** *abroad.*
**Vsheqwonnaih,** *hair of a deer.* Bodl. **vshegwunnaih.**
**Vshvccohomen,** *to beat corn into meal.*
**Vskepewh,** *to come quickly.*
**Vskepijah,** *to come quickly.*

**Vsketehamū**, *meal made of gynny wheat.* Bodl. **usketehamun**.

**Vsocan**, *gristle of a sturgeon.*

**Vsowcunnemū**, *to pour in water.* Bodl. **vsowcunnemun**.

**Vspeuwh**, *above.* Bodl. **vspevwh**.

**Vsquion**, *arrow.*

**Vsqwaseins**, *girl.*

**Vsqwasenis oc**, *girls.*

**Vsqwausum**, *bitch.*

**Vsqwÿh**, *above.* Bodl. **vsgwiih**.

**Vssac**, *crane.*

**Vsseqwahamun**, *to rub; smooth* (Bodl.).

**Vtacaskis**, *lizard or eft.*

**Vtacqwowsun**, *to come up.*

**Vtagwoong**, *stinging of a snake.*

**Vtahtahamū**, *to put out a candle.* Bodl. **vtahtahamun**.

**Vtakaer**, *to sacrifice.* Bodl. **vtakar**.

**Vtakijk**, *next.*

**Vtanneqwun**, *to suit one's nose.* Bodl. **vtannegwan**.

**Vtchappoc**, *root.* Bodl. **vtchapoc**.

**Vtcharund**, *before.*

**Vtcheiks**, *the north.*

**Vtchepetaiuwh**, *curled hair.*

**Vtchepitchewain**, *to tell a lie.*

**Vtchepwoissuma**, *east.* Bodl. **vtchepwoissvnna**.

**Vtchoonggwai**, *a cat or wild beast much bigger and spotted black under the belly as a luzarne.*

**Vtmoiahken**, *to let anything fall.* Bodl. **vtamocahken**.

**Vtshecommuc**, *chamber*.
**Vtshemaijn**, *beneath*. Bodl. **vtshemaiin**.
**Vtshemandgij**, *underneath*. Bodl. **vtshemaijnd**.
**Vtshowwah**, *the stones of any male thing, testicles*. (Bodl.)
**Vtsseneind**, *to do so*.
**Vtssetecuttawsew**, *to beat any iron to an edge*.
**Vttacawai**, *lion*. Bodl. **vttacawoi**.
**Vttacomaik**, *a codfish*. (Bodl.)
**Vttamainquoih**, *purse*.
**Vttamancoch**, *bag*.
**Vttamancoih**, *tobacco bag*.
**Vttapaantam**, *a deer*. Bodl. **vttapantam**.
**Vttassantassowaih**, *stranger*. Bodl. **vttasantassawaih**.
**Vttawh**, *mortar*.
**Vtteitsouk**, *a whiting*.
**Vttocannuc**, *wing*. Bodl. **vttacomac**.
**Vtucotucosa**, *to roll or toss as a ship*.
**Vtumpseis**, *old woman*.
**Vummewsun**, *to stir oneself*.
**Vummatahamū**, *to stir the pot*. (Bodl.)
**Vummaskittuwh**, *to go to stool or to ease oneself*. (Bodl.)
**Vummaumum**, *to take up*. (Bodl.)
**Vunamun**, *to see*.
**Vusshebowskeom**, *to stretch oneself*. (Bodl.)
**Vwwap**, *to hurt, or a thing that hurts me*.
**Vyaucopen**, *to drink to one*. Bodl. **vnaucopen**.
**Vyvnnecussopisson**, *to scratch one's head*. Bodl. **vnvnecussopisson**.

**Wahchesao,** *nest of a bird.*
**Wamattuwh,** *it is well or enough.*
**Wapapammdge,** *vine.*
**Wapewh,** *cut or a hurt.*
**Wapin,** *a stab.*
**Warnat,** *enough.*
**Wawapunnah,** *to hang one.*
**Wawirak,** *horns of a deer.*
**Wecacke,** *yard of a raccoon.*
**Wehsacanoc,** *the fur of the beast arrathcune* [raccoon]. Bodl. **wessacanoc.**
**Weihkippeis,** *hemp.*
**Weihsatonowans,** *beard.*
**Weihtaooes,** *ears of a hare or any other beast.* Bodl. **weihtaws.**
**Weimb,** *marrow of a bone.*
**Weisacannac,** *skin of a hare.*
**Weiskis,** *a place.*
**Wekowehees,** *hare.*
**Weputtahoc,** *a stake.*
**Wesaws,** *younger.* Bodl. **wesums.**
**Weyans,** *lean.*
**Wiaaws,** *the lean of any flesh.*
**Wijhcats,** *fins of a fish.*
**Wijchaudg,** *fingernails.* (Bodl.)
**Wijhcutteis,** *hare.*
**Wijhtoram,** *pike.* Bodl. **kijhtoroon.**
**Wijhwaivwh,** *blunt.*

**Winamaik,** *a small fish as big as a roach.* (Bodl.)
**Windscup,** *lead.*
**Wingaivwh,** *glorious, smooth, beautiful.*
**Wingam outssemetsumneic,** *my foot is well.* Bodl. **wingan outssemetsumneir**.
**Wingan,** *good.*
**Winganouse,** *very good.*
**Wingapo,** *welcome, or the word of greeting.*
**Wingatewh,** *ripe.*
**Winggapo,** *my beloved friend.*
**Wingutscaho,** *better.*
**Wingutsee upooc,** *the tobacco is good.* Bodl. **wingutseo vhpooc**.
**Winpe,** *marrow.*
**Wintuc,** *a fool.*
**Wintuccum,** *a fool.*
**Wiowah,** *husband.*
**Wiraohawh,** *fat.* Bodl. **wiroakawh**.
**Wiroance,** *a king or great lord.* Bodl. **wiroans**.
**Wironausqua,** *queen, a woman queen.* Bodl. **wiroansqua**.
**Wmgan,** *good.*
**Wmpenton,** *cuckold.* Bodl. **wimpenton**.
**Wnijqwans,** *a thigh.* Bodl. **wiihgwaus**.
**Wohaikank,** *scales of a fish.* Bodl. **wohaihank**.
**Woock,** *caviar.*
**Woock,** *roe of sturgeon.*
**Woor,** *hole.*
**Wopussouc,** *swan.*

**Woskan,** *a bone.* Bodl. **wuskan**.
**Woskeqwus,** *the gills of a sturgeon or any other fish.*
**Woughtathe,** *swim.*
**Wousckan,** *a bone.* Bodl. **wouscan**.
**Woussicket,** *running brook.*
**Wouwh,** *egg.* Bodl. **wovwh**.
**Wushaqwun,** *the swingle of a deer, tail.* Bodl. **wushagwun**.
**Wysotonoans,** *beard.* Bodl. **wisotonoans**.

**Yapam,** *the sea.*
**Yeahaukan,** *house.* Bodl. **yeahawkan**.
**Yeokanta,** *river.*
**Yeough,** *four.*
**Yoaxvwh,** *yonder, far off.* Bodl. **yoaruwh**.
**Yocaanta,** *river.*
**Yohacan,** *house.*
**Yoowah,** *he.*
**Yowhs,** *these.*
**Yowhse,** *hard by.*
**Yowkk,** *this.*

**Zanckone,** *to sneeze.*

# ENGLISH—POWHATAN

**Above**, *oskeitch*, *vspeuwh*, *vsqwÿh*.
**Abroad**, *vscound*.
**Ache, my legs ache**, *vnegapamutta mennetatakij*.
**Acorn**, *anaskimmins*.
**Acorns**, *anaskomens*.
**Adder**, *keihtascooc*, *sassacomuwah*.
**Afternoon**, *aunshecapa*.
**Ague**, *chowhwasuw*.
**Air**, *rarascaū*.
**Alive**, *kekewh*.
**All**, *cheisk*.
**Alone**, *apopaqwatecus*.
**Angle**, *aamowk*.
**Angry**, *perervimuw*.
**Apple**, *maracah*.
**Apron or any kind of dressed leather**, *mataheigh catommoik*.
**Arm**, *mese*.
**Arm, the**, *muckatahone*.
**Arms**, *meascoh*.
**Arrow**, *asqweowan*, *vsquion*.
**Arrowhead**, *raputtak*. **Arrowhead that is round**, *assamuwh*.
**Arse**, *kensekit*.
**Ashes**, *pungwe*, *punguy*.
**Asleep, I have been asleep**, *mummascushenepo*.
**Aunts**, *ariqwossac*.
**Autumn**, *punsaos*.

**Awake,** *aumaumer.*
**Away,** *keij.*
**Awl,** *pocohack.* **Awl pin,** *pocohaac.*
**Aye,** *nim.*

**Bachelor,** *matawiowijh.*
**Bag,** *porasap, vttamancoch.*
**Bald,** *paatchkiscaw.*
**Ball,** *aitowh.*
**Bark, to,** *cuttoundg.*
**Barrel,** *ohtamocan.*
**Basket,** *manote.* **Make a basket,** *mannottaihcaun.*
**Beads, blue,** *vnetagwushomon.*
**Beak,** *mehkewh.*
**Beans,** *peccatoas, peketawes.*
**Bear,** *amonsoquath, momonsacqweo.*
**Beard,** *weihsatonowans, messetonaance, wysotonoans.*
**Beast like a fox,** *arathkone.* **Beast in bigness like a pig and in taste alike,** *aposon.* **A beast so called,** *mussane.*
**Beat out with a cudgel,** *auntemdun, nooueshetun.* **To beat a thing with a hammer,** *suttecahamun* (Bodl.). **To beat corn into meal,** *vshvccohomen.* **To beat any iron to an edge,** *vtssetecuttawsew.*
**Beautiful,** *muscaivwh, wingaivwh.*
**Beaver,** *pohkevwh.*
**Bed,** *cawwaivwh, petacawin.* **Make a bed,** *ouronnemunpeta cawwin* (Bodl.)
**Been, I have been,** *nearnowwan.*

**Before**, *vtcharund*.
**Beggar**, *cuttassamais*.
**Behind**, *taangoqwaÿk*.
**Bell**, *maucaqwins*.
**Bells, small**, *maquiquins*.
**Below**, *nousomon*.
**Bench**, *tussan*.
**Bend, to**, *accongaivwh*. **Not to bend**, *sansaqivawwh*.
**Beneath**, *vtshemaijn*.
**Berries, blue berries of the bigness of grapes very pleasant**, *accoondews*.
**Better**, *wingutscaho*.
**Bill**, *mehkewh*.
**Bird**, *tshehip, tshetcheindg*. **Small bird or chicken**, *cawahcheims*. **A small bird of diverse colors**, *matassumitohook*. **Bird with carnation-colored wings**, *ahshowcutteis*. **Bird like a lapwing color gray which uses the water**, *monahamshaw*. **Divedapper bird**, *osasianticus*. **Watchet-colored bird**, *ockquins*.
**Bitch**, *vsqwausum*.
**Bite, to**, *amin, nussacum*.
**Black**, *mahcatawaiuwh*. **To paint black**, *nummatchqwran* (Bodl.), *mahcataowh* (Bodl.).
**Blew**, *osaih*. (—blue?)
**Blind**, *nehpaangunnū*.
**Block**, *taccahooc*.
**Blossom of a black cherry**, *amkonning*. (Bodl.)
**Blow anything**, *nepotatamen*. **Blow the fire with your mouth**, *powtowhone boketan*.

**Blunt**, *wijhwaivwh*. **To make blunt**, *neihpunsannvwh*.
**Board**, *cutsotahwooc*.
**Boat**, *acomtan, kayquiose*. **Little boat**, *aquintayne taux*. **Small boat**, *aquointan*. **Make a boat**, *cowcacunnenuñ, ahtowvun*.
**Bob of the gynny wheat without corn**, *okisher, okinsher*.
**Bodkin**, *pocohack*.
**Boil up**, *potopotawh tawh*.
**Bone, a**, *woskan, wousckan*.
**Bottle**, *poheewh*.
**Bow**, *auhtab, hawtoppe*.
**Bowstring**, *auppes, aupeis*.
**Box in which they play a certain kind of game**, *assowpook*.
**Boy**, *vcsapess*. **Young boy**, *meroathachessum*.
**Bramble**, *cawmdguc*.
**Brant**, *oyykerough*.
**Braser**, *qwunnumsc*.
**Brass**, *osawas*.
**Bread**, *apones, appoans*. **Bread made of a woat called**, *taccaho appoans*. [woat = oat? or wheat?] **To make bread**, *apoanocanosutch*.
**Break with one's fingers**, *vdesinamun*. **To break all in pieces**, *ketarowksumah*. **To break by striking**, *paskeaw, vdeistahamū*. **To break a stick**, *vnchgucheis caumelmushe*. (Bodl.)
**Breast of a woman**, *otaus*.
**Briar**, *cawmdguc*.
**Bridge**, *metucs*.

**Bright or plain all over**, *muscaussum*.
**Bring**, *peache*. **To bring into the boat**, *paaksetower*. **To bring again**, *patow*.
**Broil bread**, *apetawh poan*.
**Broken or cracked**, *perew*. **Naught broken or cracked**, *perewh* (Bodl.)
**Brook, running**, *woussicket*.
**Broom**, *tshekehicawwuns*.
**Broth**, *noumpqwaam*.
**Brother**, *nemat, kemotte*.
**Bruise anything small**, *vnetawvnnū*.
**Brush, a**, *vnepawahumā*.
**Burn, I burn**, *kuttchawe*. **To burn as if a shake light on anything**, *cutchow matowran*.
**Butterfly**, *manaang-gwas*.
**By and by**, *husque*.


**Call, to**, *otassapnar*. **What do you call this?**, *caqwaih* (Bodl.), *cacuttewaas yowk* (Bodl.).
**Calm**, *cohqwaivwh*.
**Can or any such thing to drink in**, *oktamocan*.
**Candle or gummy stick which will keep light**, *osanintak*.
**Cane**, *nisake*.
**Canoe**, *aquointan, aquintayne taux*.
**Cap**, *puttaiqwapisson*.
**Capsize**, *cotappesseaw*.
**Care, I care not for it**, *nummaskatamen*.
**Carry a thing up and down**, *nawwiowashim*. **To carry a**

thing between two, *necussagwns*. **To carry upon one's shoulder**, *ahcohkinnemun*.

**Cast, to**, *nummeraantaan* (Bodl.)

**Cat or wild beast much bigger, and spotted black under the belly as a luzarne**, *vtchoonggwai*.

**Catch in the mouth as dogs do**, *onascandamen, opassontamen*.

**Caviar**, *woock*.

**Cedar**, *maraak, moroke*.

**Chain**, *rarenaw*. **Chain of copper with long links**, *tapaantaminais*.

**Chamber**, *vtshecommuc*.

**Cheese**, *ootun*.

**Chest**, *pacus*.

**Chestnuts**, *opommins, opomens*.

**Chew, to**, *tawhtagwountamen*.

**Chicken**, *cawahcheims*.

**Child**, *nechaun, nechañ*.

**Chop wood**, *catchcahmun mushe*.

**Circle**, *mussetaqwaioh*.

**Civet cat**, *attowrin*.

**Clap one's hands**, *passahicaan*.

**Claw of a crab**, *ohtindge*.

**Clay**, *pussagwuñ*. **The clay they make pipes of**, *asasqueth*.

**Cleanse a pipe**, *jacuttehwoon*. **To cleanse the ground and make it fit for seed**, *monascunnemū*.

**Cleave, to**, *auputchahgwetaw*. (Bodl.)

**Climb a tree**, *ahcoushe*.

**Clouds**, *mammaum, arrahqwotuwh.*
**Coal of fire**, *mahcatois.*
**Coat**, *mantchoor.*
**Coat of plate**, *aqwahussun.*
**Cobweb**, *muttassapec.*
**Cockle**, *osakescai.*
**Codfish**, *ouhshawkowh, vttacomaik.* (Bodl.)
**Cold**, *nonssamats.* **I am cold**, *curcye neire.*
**Comb**, *reihcoan, rickahone.*
**Come, to come, being spoken familiarly or hard by**, *caumorowath, caumeir, caumear-ah.* **To come, being spoken afar off to one**, *pijah, pijarowah, pijarah.* **Come again**, *oiacpijann, naantuc-ah, pijautch.* **We will come again**, *oiacpijannn, naantuc-ah, pijautch.* **Come quickly**, *vskepijah, vskepewh.* **Come down**, *neighsawhor.* **Come in**, *peintiker.* **Come up**, *vtacqwowsun.* **I will come tomorrow**, *neihpyahraiab* (Bodl.)
**Command, I am at your**, *netab, netapewh.*
**Companion, your**, *numerothequier.*
**Copper**, *matassuñ.*
**Cord**, *pemuntnaw, pemanataon.*
**Corn, parched corn ground small**, *rokohamin.*
**Cough, to**, *nussuccum.*
**Cover one**, *ahgwur.*
**Covering or mantle made of feathers**, *cawassow; puttawus* (Bodl.)
**Crab**, *tuttascuc.*
**Crack**, *chakasowe, paskasew, tatumsew.*

**Cracked,** *paskasew, tatumsew, perew.* **Naught broken or cracked,** *perewh* (Bodl.)

**Crane,** *vssac.*

**Creek,** *meihsutterask.*

**Crooked,** *ohorinne.*

**Crow,** *ohawas.*

**Crown,** see **king of the head.**

**Crown of deers' hair dyed red,** *cutaantaqwapissun.* (Bodl.)

**Crows, the cock crows,** *moninaw, cutsecammo.*

**Crumb,** *towaughe.*

**Cry, to,** *neighseum.*

**Cuckold,** *wmpenton.*

**Curded matter made of milk,** *ootun.*

**Cut, to,** *vnekishemū.* **Cut the hair of a man's head,** *moundg, nummundgū, cummundgū.* **Cut rushes,** *maniasc cake.*

**Cut or a hurt,** *wapewh.*


**Dance, to,** *kantokan, cante-cante.*

**Dare, I dare not,** *necqurissar, nequtahke.*

**Dark,** *pahcunnaioh.*

**Daughter,** *amosens.*

**Day,** *cuttepacus, raieawk.*

**Dead,** *tsepaih.* **I am dead,** *nepunche neir.*

**Deaf,** *cuppotaw.*

**Deep over the head,** *nuttahcaam.* **Deep to the middle,** *tsaqwomoi.*

**Deer, a,** *vttapaantam.*
**Deer, single of a,** *wushaqwun.*
**Devil, the,** *riapoke, riokosick.*
**Dirt,** *keshackaivwh.*
**Dish, a,** *outacan.* **Make a dish,** *ackohican.*
**Dive, to,** *poohkewh.* **Dive underwater,** *pokin, pokeyough.*
**Divedapper bird,** *osasianticus.*
**Divide a thing in half,** *rickewh.*
**Do, to,** *noungat.* **To do so,** *vtsseneind.*
**Dog,** *attemous, attomois.*
**Doublet,** *mantchoor.*
**Dram,** *ahqwohhooc.*
**Drink,** *vmpsemen apook.*
**Drink, to drink to one,** *vyaucopen, kucopen.* **I would drink,** *vgaucopessum.* **I drink to you,** *kawkopen quier.* **I will drink no more,** *nutsseqwacup.*
**Drink,** *vmpsemen apook.*
**Dry by fire or otherwise,** *gaukenates, tsetewh.*
**Duck,** *piscoend, pisquaon.*
**Dust,** *nepensun.*
**Dwell, to,** *nahapuc.*
**Dye, red,** *pohcoons, poughkone, mataquiwun.*

**Eagle,** *opotenaiok.*
**Ears, the,** *metawke.* **Ear, of a man,** *meihtawk.* **Ears of a hare or any other beast,** *weihtaooes, mechijn.*
**Ear of wheat,** *autowtaoh.* **Ear of new wheat,** *maucatawatsomeon.*

**Earth**, *aspamū, ottawm, chippsin.*
**East**, *vtchepwoissuma.*
**Eat, to**, *mecher, pasquehamon.* **I will eat**, *nummechijn.*
  **I'll eat by and by**, *mechocusk.* **Eat with me**, *meihtussuc.*
  **You eat**, *minchin quire, minchin.*
**Eel**, *ascamauk.*
**Eft**, *vtacaskis.*
**Egg**, *wouwh, owaugh.*
**Eight**, *nuscawes.*
**Elbow**, *meisquan.*
**Elder**, *nussaandg.*
**Elements, the**, *poomp arrathqwatuwh.*
**Enemy**, *macherew, marapo.*
**Enough**, *warnat, neimbat.*
**Entombing**, *paiamasuw.*
**Eye, the**, *muskiendguk.* **The eyes**, *muskiendues, muskins.*

**Face, the**, *vscaentur.*
**Faint, to be faint**, *nettencrianges, nummamuntam.*
**Fall, to**, *ammawskin, adamoin, adamosū.* **To be like to fall**, *cawesewh.* **Fall down from a tree**, *raqwassewhmushe.* **To let anything fall**, *vtmoiahken.*
  **Fall of a tree**, *penim.*
**Fall of the leaf**, *punsaos.*
**Falls at the upper end of the king's river**, *paqwachowng.*
**Far off**, *oughrath, yoaxvwh.*
**Farewell**, *anath.* **Farewell, or the word at parting**, *anah.*
**Fart, a**, *poket.*

**Fat**, *wiraohawh*.
**Father**, *nows, kowse*.
**Fawn**, *nonattewh*.
**Feathers**, *ahpewk*. **A long feather**, *meqwanoc*. **Feathers of an arrow**, *assaovnsawh*.
**Feed with a spoon**, *accopaatamun*.
**Feet**, *messetts*. **Feet of a hawk**, *oremgeis*.
**Fetch**, *peache*. **Fetch some fire**, *meshpataan bocotaoh*.
**Fight at fisticuffs**, *nummecaxuttenax*.
**Fill the pipe with tobacco**, *bmseran apook*.
**Filthy**, *moieh, moiowat*.
**Finger, the fore finger**, *nummeisutteingwah*. **The long finger**, *nuttawwuttemdg*. **The ring finger**, *nowqweitut*. **The little finger**, *nummeisutteidg*. **The fingers**, *meteingeies* (Bodl.)
**Fingernails**, *wijchaudg* (Bodl.)
**Fins of a fish**, *wijhcats*.
**Fire**, *boketawh, bocuttaw*. **A coal of fire**, *mahcatois*. **A spark of fire**, *accecow, pahquarra*. **To make a fire**, *socaquinchenimum, neusakaqwan*. **The fire is out**, *otawiaac bocataw*.
**Fish**, *nammais, namaske, nameche*. **A small fish as big as a roach**, *winamaik* (Bodl.)
**Fishhook**, *auketuttawh, mowhkohan*.
**Five**, *porance*.
**Flame**, *catzahanzamusheis*.
**Flax**, *tshehaoah*.
**Flea, a**, *nuttaqwon*.
**Flee, to**, *poshenaan*.

**Flip with one's finger**, *vnepasknoterahbon*. (Bodl.)

**Flour**, *rouhcat, rowsewh*.

**Flower of the apple maraccih**, *tsemahcaug*. **A flower of a fine thing**, *muskaivwh* (Bodl.)

**Fly, a**, *mowchesoh, mowcheson*.

**Fly, to**, *awassew, bauqweuwh*.

**Fool, a**, *wintuc, wintuccum*.

**Foot, the**, *messeate*. **My foot is well**, *wingam outssemetsumneic*.

**Forehead, the**, *muskan*.

**Forget, I have forgotten**, *noewanathsoun*.

**Four**, *yeough*.

**Fowl like a teale with a sharp bill like a blackbird**, *ceumcats*. **Waterfowl in bigness of a duck, finely colored with a copit crown**, *meihteams*. **Fowl like a goose or brant**, *oyykerough*. **A fowl in likeness of a [?] footed with a sharp beak**, *tshoegetewh* (Bodl.)

**Fox**, *assimoest, onxe*.

**Frame, make a**, *cowcacunnenuñ, ahtowvun*.

**Free, I give it you free**, *thaigwenvmmeraan*.

**Friend, or the principal word of kindness**, *netab*. **I am your friend**, *netab, netapewh*. **My dear friend**, *netap*. **My beloved friend**, *winggapo*. **All friends**, *cheskchamay*.

**Frost**, *tacqwacat*.

**Froth**, *peihtaoh*.

**Full, to be full**, *geispun*. **I am full**, *negeisp*.

**Fur like a sable's**, *tangeqwath*. **Fur of the beast arratheune [raccoon]**, *wehsacanoc*.

**Gape**, **to**, *tawatuttener*.
**Garden**, *oronocah*.
**Garfish**, *tatamaho*.
**Garter**, *kispurracautapus*.
**Gate**, *cuppenauk*.
**Get you gone**, *keij*.
**Gills of a sturgeon or any other fish**, *woskeqwus*.
**Girdle**, *bagwanchy basson, pokontats, nepogwaanshepissun* (Bodl.)
**Girl**, *vsqwaseins*.
**Girls**, *vsqwasenis oc*.
**Girth, that girds their middles**, *maangwaoap*. (Bodl.)
**Give**, **to**, *paatch-ah, pasemeh*. **Give it to me**, *tangoa*. **Give it to him**, *cummeish yoowah*. **Give me a little piece**, *kapessemapaangun*. **I will not give it**, *malacommeir*. **Give this to the child**, *meishmicoan chessoyowk*. **Give me some tobacco**, *paseme vppooke*. **Give me some water**, *mammahe sucqwahum*. **Give me some meat**, *meishnahmecher*. **Give me some butter or fat to spread on my bread**, *paatch nah rungan vdamushcan*. **You gave it to me**, *komeratimiere quier* (Bodl.)
**Glorious**, *muscaivwh, wingaivwh*.
**Glove**, *oteingas, oteincas*. **A shooting glove**, *mereengass* (Bodl.)
**Glue or gum that fastens on their arrow heads**, *vppeinsaman*.
**Gnat**, *poenguwh*.

**Go, to**, *ireh, paspeen*. **Go up**, *accowson*. **Go down**, *ireh cuppeintanaan*. **Go abroad**, *ireh vscoend*. **Go along**, *cawcawmear, ascamaner*. **Go in**, *vscomtain*. **Go softly**, *vdasemeodaan*. **Go home**, *nummacha*. **Go before**, *nepopawinin*. **Go after**, *apahhammundg*. **Now let's go together**, *caumenaan, cowichawwotun*. **The ships go home**, *vppoushun mushower*. **Let us go or come away**, *ioughqueme wath*. **I will go home**, *nummacha*. **Will you go home**, *numma*.

**God**, *ahone, rawottonemd*.

**Gone**, *maentchatemayoac*. **Not gone up**, *kekenohaivwh vspewh*. **Get you gone**, *keij*.

**Good**, *wmgan, wingan*. **Very good**, *winganouse*.

**Good morrow, or the word of salutation**, *kencuttemaum*.

**Goose**, *kahangoc, kahunge*.

**Gosling**, *marahungoc*.

**Gourd**, *mahawke, pamyauk*.

**Grain**, *rassewocatuwh*. (Bodl.) **A kind of grain to eat**, *chichiquāmins*.

**Grapes**, *marrakimmins*. **Bunch of grapes**, *metucsmarakimmins*.

**Grass**, *mehteqweins*.

**Grasshopper**, *tatacaunshewah*.

**Gratis, I give it you gratis**, *thaigwenvmmeraan*.

**Grave**, *ourcar*. **Make a grave**, *cuttahamunourcar*.

**Great**, *mangoite; rummotaihwh* (Bodl.) **A great deal**, *moowchick*. **A great way**, *amaiuwh, netacoon*.

**Gristle of a sturgeon**, *vsocan*.

**Ground**, *petawin*.
**Grow high, to**, *otsetuns*, *cutterewh*.
**Gull**, *coiahqwus*.
**Gum that fastens on their arrow heads**, *vppeinsaman*. **The gum that issueth out of a certain tree called the Virginian maple**, *pickewh*. **The gum we hold balsome**, *pickutts*.
**Gun**, *pacussac-an*, *pokosack*.
**Gust**, *tohtummocunnum*.
**Guts**, *otakeisheheis*.
**Gynny wheat**, *pohcuwtoah*, *pacussacan* (Bodl.) **The stalk of gynny or Virginia wheat**, *thepahcoon* (Bodl.)


**Hair of the head**, *merersc*. **Curled hair**, *vtchepetaiuwh*, *awrewhmerersk*. **Hair of a deer**, *vsheqwonnaih*.
**Hand**, *metmge*. **A hand**, *meihtinge*.
**Hang one**, *wawapunnah*.
**Hard**, *esepannuwh*.
**Hard by**, *yowhse*.
**Hare**, *wijhcutteis wekowehees*.
**Hat**, *pattihquapisson*, *puttaiqwapisson*.
**Hatchet**, *taccahacan*, *tamahaac*, *tamohake*. **An Indian hatchet**, *cunsenagwus*.
**Have, to**, *nohaivwh*. **I have it**, *nahayhough*. **I have it not**, *mattanahayyough*, *mayanse*. **Who has this**, *owanough*. **He has not**, *tahmocassewh*. **He has none**, *tahmocassewh*. **I have none**, *mahmaindg-nohaivwh*.
**Hazelnut**, *paaugahtamuns*.

**He,** *yoowah.*

**Head, the,** *mintabukhan.* **Head of a man,** *mendabuccah.* **Head, of an arrow,** *raputtak.* **Head of an arrow that is round,** *assamuwh.*

**Headache,** *kawmdvppaan.*

**Hear, to,** *nowwuntamen.* **Not to hear,** *mata-nowwontamen.*

**Hearing,** *aumpsuwk.*

**Heaven,** *mounshaqwatuwh.*

**Heed, take,** *amuwoir.*

**Height, of a little,** *tangasuw.* **Height of anything at a good growth,** *mangeker.*

**Hell,** *popogwussur.*

**Hemp,** *weihkippeis.*

**Here,** *miske.*

**Hide or cover from the rain,** *cushe.*

**Hill,** *romuttun, pomotawh.*

**Hold it aside,** *hatacqwoear.* **Take hold of,** *mammun.*

**Hole,** *woor.* **Great hole,** *maangairagwatowh.* **To make a hole,** *mbococotamen.*

**Horns of a deer,** *wawirak.*

**Hose, I have no hose,** *matacawqweowanneth.*

**Hot weather,** *vneshawocanassup.* **It is hot weather,** *chingissum.*

**House,** *yohacan, yeahaukan.* **Great house,** *machacammac.*

**How many,** *keis.*

**Hungry,** *noiatewk, vnapootain.* **I am hungry,** *howghweyh takon neire.*

**Hurricane,** *tohtummocunnum.*

**Hurt, to,** *ahkij, vwwaap.* **It hurts me not,** *mamoindgakij, potterakai.* **A thing that hurts me,** *ahkij, vwwaap.* **I hurt my leg,** *vnechacuskonahsa* (Bodl.) **It hurts my legs,** *vnegapamutta mennetatakij.*
**Husband,** *wiowah.*
**Husk of their wheat,** *pocututauha.*


**I,** *near.*
**Ice,** *oreih.*
**Island,** *memnunnahqus.*
**Itch,** *vnechikutchikussa.*

**Jags of the savages' habit,** *rassawans.*
**Jerkin,** *mantchoor.*
**Jeron stone,** *penonge.*


**Keel, to,** *nindgvttecohcapar* (Bodl.)
**Keep, I must keep it,** *nuwamatamen.*
**Kettle, copper,** *aucutgaqwassan.*
**Kettle,** *aucogwins.*
**Kick, to,** *keiskecamon.*
**King,** *wiroance, veroanee.*
**King's name of Roanoke,** *nanamachauwh.*
**King of the head,** *nindgapamutla mecreentecoh.* **A king of the teeth,** *vneghiawmdupmeputs.* [crown?]
**Kiss, to,** *tsepaantamen.*
**Kixe,** *atapahañ, natapahan.*
**Knife,** *damisac, rekasque.*

**Knock, to knock a thing with a hammer,** *suttecahamun* (Bodl.) **To knock upon one's finger it being pricked,** *vsasarouhketahamū* (Bodl.)
**Knot, to knot up hair they tie upon their heads,** *vdansqwapissun.*
**Know, I know not,** *kanyough.*

**Ladle,** *hamkone, tshepoijn.*
**Lame,** *nepawironowh.*
**Lamprey,** *rahtaws.*
**Land,** *chippsin, cheipsin.*
**Landsmen,** *pachimoina* (Bodl.)
**Laugh, to,** *kesshekissum.*
**Lay down a thing,** *nawhpomind.*
**Lazy, I am lither or lazier,** *mushawwacat.*
**Lead,** *windscup.*
**Leaf of a prickle pear,** *matakuske.*
**Lean of the flesh,** *oiawh, wiaaws.*
**Lean,** *weyans.* **Lean against,** *atcheisqwansun.* **Lean to,** *atcheisqwansun.*
**Leap, to,** *huspissaan.* **To leap as men leap in dancing, or otherwise,** *netuspus.*
**Leather,** *uttocais.* **Leather strips or strings,** *rahsawans.* **Leather that covers their hips and privates,** *paqwantawun.* **Leather that girds their middles,** *maangwaoap.* (Bodl.)
**Leaves,** *maangwipacus.* **Dead leaves,** *moincaminge.*
**Leg, the,** *meskott.* **My legs ache,** *vnegapamutta mennetatakij.*

**Lice, you have no**, *matavtapawpeak*.
**Lie, to tell a**, *vtchepitchewain*.
**Lie down to sleep**, *machenecawwun*. **Lie together**, *cowijhpaantamū*. **Lie with a woman**, *saccasac*.
**Lift up, to**, *vdespunnemun*.
**Light**, *keshawtewh*.
**Light, to**, *iaheasomaw*. **It is not lighted**, *matackesa*.
**Lightning**, *kecuttannowas*.
**Line, small**, *pemanataon*.
**Linen**, *matassaih*.
**Lion**, *vttacawai*.
**Lips**, *nusshaih*.
**Little**, *tanx*.
**Little, a**, *taux*.
**Lizard**, *vtacaskis*.
**Lobster**, *assahampehooke, ahshaham*.
**Long**, *cunnaivwh*.
**Look, come look at my head**, *kenorockonoren quire*. **To look one's head**, *cuttaheum meis*. **Look asquint**, *perrmgqwak*.
**Lord, great**, *wiroance*.
**Lost**, *nowwanus*.
**Louse**, *metacum*.
**Love, I love it**, *nuwamatamen*. **I love you**, *nouwmais*. **You love**, *commomais*.
**Low**, *machess*.

**Maggot,** *mowsah.*

**Make bread,** *apoanocanosutch.* **Make a spoon,** *ampconomindg.* **Make a frame or boat,** *cowcacunnenuñ, ahtowvun.* **Make a grave,** *cuttahamunourcar.* **Make a basket,** *mannottaihcaun.* **Make a dish,** *ackohican.* **Make a mat,** *chessunnaansun.* **Make a bed,** *ouronnemunpeta cawwin* (Bodl.)

**Make fast, to,** *cuspurn.*

**Man,** *nimatewh.* **Married man,** *nowiowijh wiowah.* **Old man,** *rawerunnuwh.* **Great man,** *veroanee.* **A man's privates,** *pocohaac..*

**Maneaters,** *mussaangegwah.*

**Mariner,** *cheiksew.*

**Marrow,** *winpe.* **Marrow of a bone,** *weimb.*

**Marten,** *mouhwacus.*

**Mat,** *ananson.* **Mat made of reeds,** *anansecoon.* **Make a mat,** *chessunnaansun.*

**Match,** *nmtawooc.*

**Meal,** *rouhcat, rowsewh.* **Meal made of gynny wheat,** *vsketehamū.*

**Meat, it is good meat,** *necoondamen.*

**Melancholy, to be,** *maskihaan.*

**Melt, to,** *pussepuffactawas.*

**Mend up the fire,** *nocmchamino boketaw.*

**Milk made of walnuts,** *pocohiquara.*

**Milk,** *mutsun.*

**Mineral stone,** *pokoranse.*

**Miss the hole,** *nembobatsoho.*

**Mole, in the ground,** *momuscken.*
**Month,** *mehtoan* (Bodl.)
**Moon,** *vmpsquoth.* **Moon, new,** *suckimma.*
**Morning,** *papasowh.* **The morning is fair,** *paspasaat vscantewh.*
**Mortar,** *taccahooc, vttawh.*
**Moth,** *mohwhaiok.*
**Mother,** *kicke, nek.*
**Mount, small,** *romuttun.*
**Mountain,** *pomotawh.*
**Mouse,** *apegwus.*
**Mouth, the,** *mettone.*
**Mulberry, a,** *muskimmins.* **Mulberries,** *paskamath.*
**Muskrat,** *osasquus.*
**Mussel shell,** *tshecomah.* **Pearl mussel shells,** *vsasqwork.*
**Myself,** *neir.*


**Nails of the fingers and toes,** *mekouse.*
**Naked,** *nepowwer.*
**Name, what is your?,** *cacutterewindg kear.* **What is his name?,** *cacutterewindg yowk.* **What is my name?,** *cacuttewindg near.*
**Napkin,** *matassaih.*
**Nay,** *matah, tah.*
**Nearby,** *patewh.*
**Neck of anything,** *nusqwoik.*
**Needle,** *pocohaac.*
**Nest of a bird,** *wahchesao.*

**Net,** *aussab, nacowns.*
**Nettle,** *mauhsaan.*
**Next,** *vtakijk.*
**Next hand,** *patewh.*
**Night,** *tapacoh, reihcawh.*
**Nine,** *kykeytawe.*
**No,** *mattath, matah, tah.*
**No more,** *tawhs.*
**Noise of a piece,** *penim.*
**None,** *rawwaiend.*
**North, the,** *vtcheiks.*
**Nose, the,** *meskew, nethkeon.*
**Nut, a ground,** *ouhopunnawk.* **Nut like a small acorn, good meat,** *chechmqwanims.*

**Oak tree,** *poawamindg.*
**Oar,** *tshemacans.*
**One,** *nekut.*
**Only one,** *naantucah-necut.*
**Open anything,** *raragwunnemun* (Bodl.), *cussotunnohaans* (Bodl.). **Open the door,** *tenuecatower, rassicokear.* **Open one's eyes,** *vdapungwaren.*
**Otter,** *pohkevwh, cuttack, rocoyhook.*
**Out, all is out,** *tashoac, metatvwh neckatam.*
**Out, away, or get you gone,** *keij.* **Out or it is plucked out,** *aumpossaish.*
**Overcast or hidden under a cloud,** *reihcahahcoik.*
**Overset, or a boat to turn keel up,** *cotappesseaw.*

**Owl**, *qwangatarask.*
**Oysters**, *cauwaih.*

**Paint, red**, *poughkone.* **To paint black**, *nummatchqwran* (Bodl.), *mahcataowh* (Bodl.). **To paint red**, *numerathguran pocoon* (Bodl.)
**Pan, frying**, *ampkone.*
**Parrot**, *maskowhinge, massacamwmdg.*
**Path, going in a**, *mayis.*
**Pearl**, *makateweygh, matacawiak.*
**Pearl mussel shells**, *vsasqwork.*
**Pears**, *assentamens.*
**Peas**, *ossantamens, otassantamens.*
**Pestle**, *pocohaac.*
**Piece, a little**, *paangun.* **Piece [gun]**, *pacussac-an.* **Piece of a pot**, *rummasvwendg.* **Piece of bread**, *rowcar appons.*
**Pigeon**, *towacqwoins.* **Wood pigeon**, *qwananats.*
**Pike**, *wijhtoram.*
**Pillow**, *ahqwass* (Bodl.)
**Pin**, *pocohaac.*
**Pinch, to**, *nepkehanaan.*
**Pipe, tobacco**, *apokan, vppocano* (Bodl.). **The pipe is foul**, *vppocanomowr* (Bodl.). **The pipe is stopped**, *opoteyough.* **The pipe is broken**, *vdeishcawunvppocan* (Bodl.). **To play on a pipe**, *pawpecoon* (Bodl.)
**Piss, to**, *shekijn.*
**Pitch, to dress or pitch a boat**, *ascahamū.*
**Place, a**, *weiskis.*

**Play at any game**, *mamantū terracan*. **To play on a pipe**, *pawpecoon* (Bodl.)

**Playster**, *akontant, nuttacoondah*.

**Plot of ground to sow corn**, *oronocah*.

**Pluck up**, *nummonnemenndus*.

**Plucked out, it is**, *aumpossaish*.

**Plum, an excellent**, *pichamnis*. **A plum very delicious when it is ripe**, *pushenims*. **Plum stone**, *maquascawnomell*.

**Polecat**, *cuttenamvwhwa*.

**Porpoise**, *potawaugh*.

**Porridge**, *noumpqwaam*.

**Post**, *meihtoram*.

**Pot**, *ancagwins*. **Little stone pot**, *hauquequins*. **A pot to drink in**, *kequasson*. **A piece of a pot**, *rummasuwendg*.

**Potsherd**, *rummasuwendg*.

**Pour out water**, *qwatshacumhcaan*. **Pour in water**, *vsowcunnemū*.

**Pox, the**, *nummagwais*.

**Prayer**, *maunomommaon*. **Come to prayer**, *pijahtamaon*

**Prisoner, take one**, *necakessuttun*.

**Privates of a man**, *pocohaac*. **Privates of a woman**, *mutusk, mocosijt*.

**Pudding, hasty**, *asapan*.

**Pull, to**, *nummavmon*. **Pull it out**, *necantuwh*. **Pull one down**, *cuttaqwocum*.

**Pumpkin, a**, *mahcawq*.

**Purple**, *ourcrewh*.

**Purse**, *vttamainquoih*.
**Put it in**, *peinder*. **Put on**, *puttohiqwosur*. **Put off**, *pussaqwunnenidg*. **Put on your hat**, *noraughtoan*. **Put out a candle**, *vtahtahamū*.


**Queen**, *wironausqua*.
**Quickly**, *husque*.


**Rain**, *kameyhan, camzowan*.
**Rainbow**, *qwannacut*.
**Rat**, *aotawk*.
**Rattle made of a gourd**, *chmgawwonawk*.
**Raw**, *ascunmewh*.
**Red paint**, *poughkone*. **To paint red**, *numerathguran pocoon* (Bodl.)
**Reed**, *nissakan, nehsaakah*.
**Rend, to**, *oteyquenimin*.
**Rent**, *tuttascwh*.
**Returning**, *peyeugh*.
**Rind of a tree like hemp**, *chesawk*.
**Ring**, *nekereinskeps*.
**Ripe**, *wingatewh*. **Not ripe**, *vscannewh*.
**Rise up**, *passagwear*.
**River**, *yocaanta, yeokanta*.
**Roast, to**, *apowssaw*.
**Robin red-breast**, *cheawanta*.
**Roe of sturgeon**, *woock*.
**Roll as a ship**, *vtucotucosa*.

**Root,** *vtchappoc.* **Root of tobacco,** *vppoo-chappoc.*
**Rope,** *penninaugh, pemuntnaw.*
**Rose,** *pussaqwembun.*
**Rose tree,** *pussaqwembunameindg* (Bodl.)
**Row, to,** *tchijmaoc.*
**Rub, to,** *vsseqwahamun.*
**Run, to,** *musken, rasannear.* **Go and run quickly,** *ire assuminge.*
**Rushes,** *cakakesqus.*

**Sacrifice, to,** *vtakaer.*
**Sad, to be,** *maskihaan.*
**Sail, a,** *tsemaosay.*
**Salt,** *sawwone.*
**Sand,** *racawh.*
**Say, to,** *kekuttun.*
**Scab,** *vmeqwussum.*
**Scales, of a fish,** *wohaikank.*
**Scratch, to,** *vnecussopisson.* **Scratch one's head,** *vyvnnecussopisson.*
**Scrub one's head,** *necutchucskuw.*
**Scum,** *peihtaoh.*
**Sea, the,** *yapam.*
**Seaman,** *cheiksew.*
**Seat, in a boat,** *tussan.*
**Seaweeds,** *ascaxasqwus.*
**Sedge,** *eskowwascus.*
**See, to,** *vunamun.* **Let me see it,** *numpenamun, tanggo, tangoa.* **Not to see,** *matanamowun* (Bodl.)

**Seeds**, *amenacacac*.

**Set, to set down anything**, *mhnomun* (Bodl.)

**Sew with a needle**, *husquamun*.

**Sharp**, *keneiwuh*.

**Shears**, *mundgtacan*.

**Sheldrake**, *rowhqwawh*.

**Shells**, *ohshaangumiemuns*.

**Shine, it shines**, *assentewcaiah*.

**Ship, a**, *mussowuxuc*. **Ship, great**, *aquintayne manggoy*.

**Shoe, a**, *chapant*. **Shoes**, *mawhcasuns*. **I have no shoes**, *matamawcasunneh*.

**Shoot, to**, *nepomotamen*.

**Short**, *tackqwaisuw*.

**Show, a**, *apquammon, machequeo*.

**Shut the door**, *kessohikear*.

**Sick, to be**, *aroummossouth*. **I am sick**, *aramiath south, neire*.

**Sing, to**, *cante-cante*. **Sing and dance**, *kantikantie*.

**Sister**, *cursine, nuckaandgum*.

**Sit down**, *nehapper, nawpin*. **Sit nearer to**, *otassotagwopur*. **Sit further**, *nehapper kupper; mussataquopur* (Bodl.)

**Six**, *camatinge*.

**Skin, a black fox skin or an overgrown sables**, *hawtorinkanaske*. **Skin of a stag**, *matchkore*. **Skin of a hare**, *weisacannac*.

**Sky**, *arrokoth*.

**Sleep**, *kawwin, nuppawē, nepaun*.

**Slowworm**, *apouscase*.
**Small**, *tanx*.
**Smell, to**, *nummeramin*.
**Smoke**, *kekepemgwah*.
**Smooth**, *muscaivwh, wingaivwh*; *vsseqwahamun* (Bodl.)
**Snail**, *pomahaum*.
**Snake**, *keihtascooc, sassacomuwah*.
**Sneeze, to**, *zanckone*.
**Snort, to**, *neqwaxulloundwun*.
**Snot**, *makique*.
**Snow**, *coan*. **It snows**, *rookewh coan*.
**Soak bread, to**, *nepokeunnamū*.
**Sore, a**, *meihkeih*.
**Soul**, *netshetsunh*.
**Sow, to**, *ammomū*. **Sow wheat**, *huskpemmo poketaws, nuttaspin*.
**Spade**, *aayxkehake*.
**Spark of fire**, *accecow, pahquarra*. **Sparks that glitter**, *pahgwurraow* (Bodl.). **The gold sparks in the sand**, *paskorath*.
**Sparrow hawk**, *fatacaumexan*.
**Spars of a house**, *meihtussan* (Bodl.)
**Speak**, *kicketen quier*. **Speak softly**, *kemaantuñ*. **Speak aloud**, *memmowchicktagwassan* (Bodl.)
**Spit, to**, *secon; tsehqwun* (Bodl.)
**Spoon, make a**, *ampconomindg*. **Take up with a spoon**, *auutsahamun*.
**Spring, the**, *suttekepacatvwh* (Bodl.)

**Spurn, to**, *keiskecamon*.
**Squirrel**, *moussomko*, *missanek*. **Flying squirrel**, *aiossapanijk*.
**Stab, a**, *wapin*.
**Stake, a**, *weputtahoc*.
**Stalk, a**, *mehtacooc*. **The stalk of gynny or Virginia wheat**, *thepahcoon* (Bodl.).
**Stand, to**, *vannatassun*.
**Star, a**, *attaanqwassuwk*.
**Steal, to**, *commotoouh*.
**Step, to**, *accowson*.
**Stick fast to a thing**, *auputchahgwetaw*. (Bodl.)
**Stinging of a snake**, *vtagwoong*.
**Stink, to**, *auutus*. **It stinks**, *ahtur*.
**Stir oneself**, *vummewsun*. **To stir the pot**, *vummatahamu* (Bodl.)
**Stockings**, *cawqweawans*.
**Stone**, *shacahocan*. **Little stone**, *mananst*. **The clear stones we gather**, *sakahooke*. **A grape's stone or the stone of any plum**, *macauqs*, *caunomel*.
**Stool**, *tauosin*. **A stool to sit upon**, *apahpun* (Bodl.). **Go to stool**, *vummaskittuwh* (Bodl.)
**Stop or put in a stopple**, *muttaqwohoons*.
**Straight**, *majawh*.
**Stranger**, *vttassantassowaih*.
**Strawberries**, *muskefkimmins*.
**Stretch oneself**, *vusshebowskeom* (Bodl.)
**Strew, to**, *nummeraantaan* (Bodl.)

**Strike, to,** *nepassingwahoon.* **Strike with a sword,** *vepacaman.* **Strike fire,** *bocata oc kok.*
**Strong,** *towawh.*
**Sturgeon,** *cuppatoan.*
**Suck, to,** *anowwoninr.*
**Suet, all kind of suet,** *rungâ.*
**Suit one's nose, to,** *vtanneqwun.*
**Summer,** *cowwotaioh.*
**Sun,** *nepausche, keshowse.*
**Sunrise,** *papasowh.*
**Sunset,** *qwunsewh.*
**Sup, to,** *meatsun.*
**Swallow, to,** *quantamum.*
**Swan,** *wopussouc.*
**Sweat, to,** *vebowchass.*
**Sweep, to,** *tsekehica.*
**Swell, to,** *cunnaqueis.*
**Swim, to,** *tooskean, tamokin, woughtathe.* **Swim as a piece of wood or feather on the water,** *puppoqwahauns.*
**Sword,** *monowhauk, monohacan.*

**Tail,** *wushaqwun.*
**Take it,** *vntowh, vndoth.* **Take hold of,** *mammun.* **Take off,** *rassunnemum.* **Take one prisoner,** *necakessuttun.* **Take tobacco,** *vespessemaanpooc.* **Take heed,** *amuwoir.* **Take up,** *vummaumum* (Bodl.). **Take up with a spoon,** *auutsahamun.*
**Target,** *amahoth, amunwhokk.*

**Tassel of a goshawk**, *ockquetath*.
**Tawny**, *nuscahsaiyam* (Bodl.)
**Tear, to**, *oteyquenimin*.
**Teeth, the**, *mepit, neputte*.
**Tell, to**, *cutterah*. **I cannot tell**, *caivwh*. **Tell me**, *kicketen quier*.
**Ten**, *koske*.
**Testicles**, *vtshowwah* (Bodl.)
**Thank, I thank you**, *kenah*.
**These**, *yowhs*.
**Thigh**, *apome*. **Thigh, a**, *wnijqwans*.
**Thirsty, to be dry or thirsty**, *paougwnssenttawh*.
**This**, *yowkk*.
**Thornbark, a**, *aumboick* (Bodl.)
**Thread**, *peymmatā, penimathatoan, pemanataon*. **A fine or small thread**, *vscook*.
**Three**, *nousough, nus*.
**Three hundred**, *nuswohcassannack* (Bodl.)
**Throat, the**, *vegwantaak*.
**Throw away, to**, *apacet*.
**Thumb, the**, *vketeqwaivtteindg*.
**Thunder**, *pettackqueth, vmdguppauk*.
**Tickle, to tickle someone**, *kekitchuchun* (Bodl.)
**Tie, to**, *cuspurn*.
**Toast or broil bread**, *apetawh poan*.
**Tobacco**, *apooke, vhpooc, vmpsemen apook*. **Light tobacco**, *iakesan apooke*. **The tobacco is good**, *wingutsee upooc*. **The tobacco is naught**, *keshemaik pooc*. **To-**

**bacco bag**, *camange, oughtamangoyth, reconack, vttamancoih*. **Tobacco pipe**, *vhpoocan*. **To take tobacco**, *vespessemaanpooc*. **I have no tobacco**, *matavppoannonuwh*. **I must put tobacco in it**, *vpococaheih*.

**Tomorrow**, *raiab, vimawh, riapoke*.

**Tongue, the**, *maxatsno*.

**Torn**, *tuttascwh*.

**Toss as a ship**, *vtucotucosa*.

**Town**, *mussaran*.

**Train of a bird**, *ottanueis*.

**Tree**, *meihtucs*. **Green tree**, *aqwataneik*. **Walnut tree**, *assunnoineindge*. **Oak tree**, *poawnncindg*.

**Turd**, *moich*.

**Turkey**, *monynawgh, monanaw*. **Turkey cock**, *ospanno*.

**Turn the coals**, *cuskessamun*.

**Turtle**, *commotins, accomodemsk*. **Sea turtle**, *tuwcuppewk*.

**Twenty**, *ningepoke*.

**Twined thread**, *pemucqweraneind*.

**Two**, *ninge*.


**Unclose hands**, *penumun*.

**Underneath**, *vtshemandgij*.

**Understand, now I understand you**, *husquequenatora*. **I understand you not**, *matagvenatoxoth, mattaquenatorath*. **I understand well**, *kennehautows*. **I understand not**, *matakennowntorawh*. **I understand you a little but not much**, *cussewh kenneaunten mata mochik*. (Bodl.)

**Vein**, a, *abescur*.
**Venison**, *rapantā*.
**Village**, *kaasun*.
**Vine**, *wapapammdge*.
**Virginia**, *Tsenahcommacah*.

**Waken, to**, *vnamun*.
**Walk, to**, *pawpawmear*. **Walk about**, *paspene*.
**Walnut**, a, *ahsmenuns, paukauns*.
**Walnuts**, *assimnims*.
**Warm, to**, *bahtanomun*. **Warm yourself**, *dawbasonquire*. **It is warm or hot weather**, *chingissum*.
**Wart**, *meihkeis*.
**Wash anything**, *ketssetawun*. **To wash the face**, *keseiqwaan*. **To wash the hand**, *keseiceindcher*.
**Water**, *suckquohana, secqwahan*. **Ebbing water**, *seiscatvwh*. **Flowing water**, *tammuscamauwh*.
**Waves, of the sea**, *aqwaskawwans*.
**Weak**, *kesshemauc*.
**Weary**, *cuttoxeen*.
**Weeds**, *attasqwas*.
**Weep, to**, *nummawh*.
**Weir to take fish**, *neihsacan*.
**Welcome or the word of greeting**, *wingapo, chamah, netab*.
**Well, it is well**, *ough, mamoindgakij, potterakai, wamattuwh*.
**Well**, a, *ohcawooc*.

**West,** *attagwassanna.*
**Wet,** *neppe.*
**What is this?,** *que quoy*; *caqwaih* (Bodl.), *cacuttewaas yowk* (Bodl.). **What is your name?,** *que quoy ternis quire.*
**Wheat,** *poketawes, pocuttawes.* **Gynny wheat,** *pohcuwtoah.* **Wheat parched in the fire,** *aparoumenans.* **Wheat plume,** *asseseim.* **The stalk of gynny or Virginia wheat,** *thepahcoon* (Bodl.)
**Whelps,** *apowhoh-homins.*
**When,** *tanoo chunck.*
**Where have you been?,** *tanaowaam.*
**Whet, to,** *nusseseqwus.*
**Whistle, to,** *qweisqwesun.*
**White,** *opaivwh.*
**Whiting, a,** *vtteitsouk.*
**Whole, it is,** *mamoindgakij, potterakai.*
**Wide,** *rummotaihwh* (Bodl.)
**Widgeon,** *ponomawus.*
**Wife,** *noungasse.*
**Wild words they have,** *mattcheroth quier, marrapoth quier* (Bodl.)
**Will, I will not,** *matush.*
**Wind,** *rassoum.*
**Wind, the,** *kikithamots.* **The small wind,** *rowhsunnvwh.* **A great wind,** *mahqwaih.*
**Wind about, to,** *pasqwuxxaws.*
**Wind up, to,** *nuwweisqwaput.*

**Wing**, *vttocannuc*.
**Wink, to**, *inspungwaren* (Bodl.)
**Winter**, *puppaannoh*.
**Wipe one's nose**, *cheiscunnemun* (Bodl.)
**Wolf**, *naantam*.
**Woman**, *crenepo, cutssenepo, cucheneppo*. **Woman with child**, *pomevwh*. **Old woman**, *vtumpseis, tumpseis*. **Woman queen**, *wironausqua*. **A woman's privates**, *mutusk, mocosijt*.
**Wonder, word of**, *vaugh*.
**Wood**, *muskeis*. **Wood all along**, *musheis-in-our-owh* (Bodl.)
**World, the**, *pamahsaivwh*.
**Worm, little**, *mowsah*.
**Wound, a**, *nepocuttokeau*.
**Wrap, to**, *nuwweisqwaput*.
**Wrestle, to**, *mamarenaretum*.
**Write, to**, *sakahocan, sekehekonaugh*.

**Yard of a raccoon**, *wecacke*.
**Yawn, to**, *tawatuttener*.
**Yea**, *cuppeh, nim*. **Yea truly**, *kouppathe*.
**Yellow**, *oussawack*.
**Yes**, *cuppeh*.
**Yesterday**, *osaioh*.
**Yonder**, *yoaxvwh*.
**You**, *kear*.
**Younger**, *wesaws*.

# Numerical Tables

## (British Museum manuscript)

1. Nekut
2. Ninge
3. Nousough *or* nus
4. Yeough
5. Porance
6. Camatinge
7.
8. Nuscawes
9. Kykeytawe
10. Koske
20. Ningepoke

## (Bodleian manuscript)

1. Nekut
2. Ninge
3. Nussaugh
4. Yeough
5. Parance
6. Camatinge
7.
8. Nuschawes
9. Kykeytawe
10. Koske
20. Ninge poke
300. Nuswohcassannack

# A POWHATAN WORD–LIST

Satterday we passed a few short reaches; and .5. mile of poore Cottage we went a shore. Heer we found our kinde Comrades again, who had gyven notice all along as they came of us: by which we were entertayned with much Courtesye in every place. We found here a Wiroans (for so they call their kynges) who satt upon a matt of Reedes, with his people about him... Certifying him of our intentyon up the Ryver, he was willing to send guydes with us. This we found to be a kyng subiect to Pawatah (the Cheife of all the kyngdomes) his name is Arahatec: the Country Arahatecoh. Now as we satt merye banquetting with them, seeing their Daunces, and taking Tobacco, Newes came that the greate kyng Powatah was come: at whose presence they all rose of their mattes (save the kyng Arahatec); separated themselves aparte in fashion of a Guard, and with a long shout they saluted him. Him wee saluted with silence sitting still on our mattes, our Captaine in the myddest; but presented (as before we dyd to kyng Arahatec) gyftes of dyvers sortes, as penny knyves, sheeres, belles, beades, glasse toyes &c. more amply then before. Now this king appointed .5. men to guyde us up the River, and sent Postes before to provyde us victuall. I caused now our kynde Consort that described the River to us, to draw it againe before kyng Arahatec, who in every thing consented to this draught, and it agreed with his first relatyon. This we found a faythfull fellow, he was one that was appointed guyde for us. Thus parting from Arahatecs ioye, we found the people on either syde the Ryver stand in Clusters all along, still proferring us victualls, which of some were accepted; as our guydes (that were with us in the boate) pleased, and gave them requitall.

—Anonymous, 1607.

**Caische**, *ten.*
**Caquassan**, *[metal or copper?].*
**Cheisc**, *all one with him or under him.*
**Matah & chirah**, *[you are bad; you are enemies?].*
**Pegatewk-apoan**, *bread made into rolls and cakes.*
**Wingapoh**, *our word of kindness.*
**Wingapoh chemuze**, *the most kind words of salutation that may be.*
**Wiroans**, *king.*
**Wisacan**, *a herb like liverwort or bloodwort which they say heals poisoned wounds.*

(the definitions in square brackets [] are supplied from context by Barbour 1969; these words are untranslated in the original text. —ed.)

# A WORD-LIST
# OF THE
# VIRGINIA INDIANS

*Of the Learning, and Languages of the* Indians.

These Indians have no sort of Letters to express their words by... Their language differs very much, as antiently in the several parts of *Britain*; so that Nations at a moderate distance, do not understand one another. However, they have a sort of general Language, like what *Lahontan* calls the *Algonkine*, which is understood by the Chief men on many Nations, as *Latin* is in most parts of *Europe*, and *Lingua Franca* quite thro the *Levant*.

The general language here us'd, is said to be that of the *Occaneeches*, tho they have been but a small Nation, ever since those parts were known to the *English*: but in what this Language may differ from that of the *Algonkines*, I am not able to determine.

—Robert Beverley, 1705.

**Cockarouse**, *great man, brave fellow; a royal councillor.*
**Cohonks**, *winter.*
**Cushaw**, *a kind of Pompion. (...of a bluish green Colour, streaked with White, when they are fit for use. They are larger than the Pompions, and have a long narrow Neck: Perhaps this may be the* Ecushaw *of T. Harriot.)*
**Cuttanimmons**, *fruit of a kind of arum. (Smith calls them* Ocoughtanamnis, *and Tehod, de Bry in his Translation,* Sacquenummener.*)*
**Hickory**, *milk.*
**Homony**, *Indian corn.*

**Kiwasa,** *their idol.*
**Macock,** *squash.*
**Maracock,** *passion flower.*
**Matchacomoco,** *grand council.*
**Match-coats,** *winter cloaks.*
**Moccasin,** *shoe.*
**Okee,** *their idol.*
**Pauwawing,** *conjuration.*
**Pawcorance,** *altar stone.*
**Peak,** *small cylinders of conch shell.*
**Pericu,** *a "Superintendent" among beavers.*
**Puccoon,** *a root (Anchuse or yellow Alkanet).*
**Quioccos,** *idol.*
**Quioccosan,** *house of religious worship.*
**Rockahomonie,** *the finest Indian corn.*
**Roenoke,** *cockleshell beads.*
**Tomahawk,** *stone hatchet.*
**Tuckahoe,** *a tuberous root.*
**Wampom peak,** *dark cylinders made of shell.*
**Werowance,** *military officer.*
**Wigwang,** *house.*
**Wisoccan,** *the practice of medicine.*
**Wysoccan,** *a mad potion.*

# CLASSIFICATION OF THE EASTERN ALGONQUIAN LANGUAGES

*Micmac*
Abenakian
    *Maliseet-Passamaquoddy*
    *Eastern Abenaki*
    *Western Abenaki*
*Etchemin*
Southern New England
    *Massachusett-Narragansett*
    *Loup*
    *Mohegan-Pequot*
    *Quiripi-Unquachog*
Delawaran
    *Mahican*
    *Munsee Delaware*
    *Unami Delaware*
*Nanticoke-Conoy*
Virginia Algonquian
    ***Powhatan***
Carolina Algonquian
    *Pamlico*

Sources: Goddard 1978; Goddard 1996.

*Also available:*

The Complete American Language Reprint Series on CD-Rom
**www.evolpub.com/ALR/ALRCDRom.html**

*and*

The Interactive ALR: An Online, Interactive Database
of Historic Native American Vocabularies and Word Lists
**www.evolpub.com/interactiveALR/home.html**

# Volumes in the ALR series

1. A Vocabulary of the Nanticoke Dialect
2. A Vocabulary of Susquehannock
3. A Vocabulary of the Unami Jargon
4. A Vocabulary of Powhatan
5. An Ancient New Jersey Indian Jargon
6. A Vocabulary of Tuscarora
7. A Vocabulary of Woccon
8. A Dictionary of Powhatan
9. A Vocabulary of Mohegan-Pequot
10. A Vocabulary of New Jersey Delaware
11. A Vocabulary of Stadaconan
12. Denny's Vocabulary of Delaware
13. A Vocabulary of Roanoke
14. Denny's Vocabulary of Shawnee
15. Cummings' Vocabulary of Delaware
16. Early Vocabularies of Mohawk
17. Schoolcraft's Vocabulary of Oneida
18. Elliot's Vocabulary of Cayuga
19. Schoolcraft's Vocabulary of Onondaga
20. Elliot's Vocabulary of Mohawk
21. Cummings' Vocabulary of Shawnee
22. A Vocabulary of Seneca
23. The Tutelo Language
24. Handy's Vocabulary of Miami
25. Observations on the Mahican Language
26. Minor Vocabularies of Tutelo and Saponi
27. Wood's Vocabulary of Massachusett
28. Chew's Vocabulary of Tuscarora
29. Early Fragments of Minsi Delaware
30. A Vocabulary of Wyandot
31. Heckewelder's Vocabulary of Nanticoke
32. Minor Vocabularies of Huron
33. Castiglioni's Vocabulary of Cherokee
34. Elements of a Miami-Illinois Grammar  (*forthcoming*)
35. Ridout's Vocabulary of Shawnee  (*forthcoming*)
39. A Vocabulary of Etchemin
40. A Vocabulary of the Souriquois Jargon

*For more information on the series, see our website at:*
**www.evolpub.com/ALR/ALRbooks.html**

CPSIA information can be obtained
at www.ICGtesting.com
Printed in the USA
FFOW02n0657280815
16356FF